Working with Support in the Classroom

Working with Support in the Classroom

Edited by Anne Campbell
and Gavin Fairbairn

P·C·P

Paul Chapman Publishing

London · Thousand Oaks · New Delhi

First published 2005

Paul Chapman Publishing
A SAGE Publications Company
1 Oliver's Yard
55 City Road
London EC1Y 1SP

SAGE Publications Inc
2455 Teller Road
Thousand Oaks, California 91320

SAGE Publications India Pvt Ltd
B-42 Panchsheel Enclave
PO Box 4109
New Delhi 110 017

Library of Congress Control Number: 2004114474

A catalogue record for this book is available from the British Library

ISBN 1 4129 0240 1
ISBN 1 4129 0241 X (pbk)

Typeset by Pantek Arts Ltd, Maidstone, Kent
Printed in Great Britain by Athenaeum Press, Gateshead

●●● Contents

●●● Preface

The time is ripe for this book. Over recent years there has been a vast increase in the number of people who support children's learning in classrooms and other educational settings, both as employees and as volunteers. In the controversial Workforce Remodelling initiative the government is planning to recruit around 50,000 teaching assistants in its efforts to raise standards and reduce workloads in education. In order to make the best and most productive use of these 'significant others' in the classroom, teachers need to have a source of advice and guidance in relation to the range of ways in which they can best collaborate with them. *Working with Support in the Classroom* will provide such a source.

Using stories of successful practice and ideas for improving collaborative work, the book explores and maps the development of the roles in relation to children's learning that can be played by people other than qualified teachers. The work of teaching assistants, learning mentors, classroom assistants for children with special educational needs, student teachers, nursery nurses and parent and community helpers are all illustrated in this book, which focuses on the whole range of educational settings from the early years through primary to secondary classrooms. Between them the editors and contributors have a wide range of experience of working in schools and early years settings with teachers and support workers, including experience in special educational needs and in work with multilingual children for whom English is a second language. It is from that experience that this book has arisen.

Anne Campbell
Gavin Fairbairn

●●● Acknowledgements

Many thanks are due to all those who, in some way or another, have supported children in their learning in all the contexts described in this book. Special debts of gratitude are due to Vicky Morten and Cath How for their help and to Ian Kane for his valuable advice and support in the editing of the book.

●●● List of contributors

Wendy Bignold is Vice Dean of Education at Liverpool Hope University College, where she leads courses in the 'Advanced study of early years', and is one of the central members of the team who have written a new pathway and foundation degree on special needs in a disabling world. Wendy has worked as a teacher in a language support service and has much experience of teaching and other educational work in the Indian subcontinent. For example, she was vice principal of a rural school in northern Pakistan, worked as an educational consultant for the Aga Khan Foundation in Tajikistan and was a consultant to the Bangladeshi government in relation to non-formal education.

Christine Bold is the Foundation Degree Director in the Education Deanery at Liverpool Hope University College. She has written *Progression in Primary Design and Technology* (David Fulton, 1999) and edited a foundation degree text for teaching assistants, *Supporting Learning and Teaching* (David Fulton, 2004). Her primary school experience included the role of the assessment co-ordinator, and she has conducted small-scale research projects on assessing learning and learning processes. She is interested in many educational issues and has extensive experience, including secondary primary, ITT, Ofsted and consultancy. Over the past three years she has been involved in developing and delivering courses for both primary and secondary teaching assistants.

Anne Campbell, Professor of Education at Liverpool Hope University College, has researched mainly in the area of teacher development. She has published in the fields of early years education and educare. She is the author, with Ian Kane, of *School-based Teacher Education: Telling Tales from a Fictional Primary School* (David Fulton, 1998) and, with Olwen McNamara and Peter Gilroy, *Practitioner Research and Professional Development in Education* (Paul Chapman Publishing, 2004). She has also published many articles about professional development in academic journals. Anne is currently leading two research and evaluation projects for the Teacher Training Agency and the National College for School Leadership.

Sue Cronin is a senior lecturer in mathematics and is a module leader on the new Liverpool Hope University College foundation degree for teaching assistants, 'Supporting learning and teaching', and she has provided various in-service courses for teaching assistants. She has published web-based materials for gifted and talented pupils for John Moores Astronomy Department and for Excellence in Liverpool.

Sue Crowley, senior lecturer, is ICT Curriculum Leader at Liverpool Hope University College. In her career in primary education, she has held senior management positions, has been an advisory teacher for ICT and co-ordinator of newly qualified teachers in Sefton. Her experience in higher education includes lecturing in primary education and ICT at Edge Hill College, Liverpool University and Liverpool Hope University College. Her publications include work for the DfES on learning mentors and ICT.

Gavin Fairbairn, Professor of Ethnics and Language at Leeds Metropolitan University, worked for many years in special education and social work before entering primary teacher education in 1985 as a senior lecturer, then Reader. He joined Liverpool Hope University College in 2002, from a chair in Professional Development in Nursing and Midwifery. He has wide-ranging research interests in education, professional ethics, health and social care. He has published many articles in education, and, in applied ethics relating to the caring professions. His book, with Chris Winch, *Reading, Writing and Reasoning* (2nd edn, Open University Press, 1996) is now in its twelfth year, and *Reading at University: A Guide for Students*, with Susan Fairbairn, was published by the Open University Press in 2001. *Integrating Special Children: Some Ethical Issues* (Avebury, 1992), which he edited with Susan Fairbairn, was published in a Polish translation by the Ministry of Education in Warsaw in 2000, and is an example of the crossover between his educational and ethical concerns.

Wendy Hall is a tutor in charge of special needs in the Education Deanery at Liverpool Hope University College, and she is currently tutoring students in Hong Kong and has supported PhD students in India. Wendy has extensive experience in the area of special needs in mainstream schools, including interagency liaison. Both her BEd and her Master's Degree focused on special needs. She holds a certificate in deaf awareness and a specialist teaching qualification in relation to dyslexia (a diploma in SpLD). She has recently written course material for the Hornsby distance learning programme.

Deirdre Hewitt taught in primary schools for 20 years before joining the staff of Liverpool Hope University College as a senior lecturer in September 2002. She has experience of working alongside students, teaching assistants and nursery nurses.

Pat Hughes is Senior Lecturer in Primary Education, Liverpool Hope University College. After a degree at Durham University, Pat worked as a social worker, pre-school playgroup worker, cleaner, laboratory assistant and FE lecturer before training to be a primary teacher. After doing this for nine years, she entered teacher training. She has been a registered Ofsted inspector, a non-executive director of Knowsley PCT and an external assessor for performance management. Pat has published many books and training packs with a number of publishers, including Heinemann, Hodder, Wayland, Nelson and David Fulton, and chapters in books published by Routledge, Paul Chapman Publishing and Multilingual Matters.

Ann-Marie Jones has recently started to work as a senior lecturer at Liverpool Hope University College, following a career in teaching nursery nurses in further education. Recently she has successfully completed her MA studies at Liverpool University and has studied partnerships between professionals in early years and nursery settings.

Mike Richardson, Senior Lecturer in ICT, is joint Head of Year 1 Education, Liverpool Hope University College. His career in education includes teaching in secondary and primary schools; work with ICL as a teacher adviser and curriculum consultant in literacy and numeracy; mentoring in schools accepting ITT students; responsibility for 'Parents in partnership' in a primary school; and lecturing in education and ICT pedagogy at Liverpool Hope University College.

Deborah Smith has recently been appointed as a senior lecturer at Liverpool Hope University College. She taught for 18 years in primary schools and has a great deal of experience working with students and nursery nurses in classrooms.

●●● Chapter 1

Introduction

Anne Campbell and Gavin Fairbairn

Over the last few years there has been a significant increase in the number of people who work in supporting children's learning in classrooms and other educational settings. Some of these people – nursery nurses, teaching assistants, learning mentors and learning support staff – are paid for their work. Others are unpaid and work as volunteers, including parents and grandparents as well as community members who aspire to a career in education and who want to gain some experience before applying for a place on an initial teacher education course, quite often on one of the more flexible routes. There are government plans to recruit another 50,000 teaching assistants in an effort to raise standards and to reduce workloads for teachers. The government's initiative to establish higher-level teaching assistants (HLTAs) (DfES, 2002) has already begun amid a flurry of controversy from teaching unions. In 2001 Nigel de Gruchy of the National Association of Schoolmasters and Union of Women Teachers, made his famous 'pig-ignorant peasants' remark, which was understood to refer to classroom assistants. His denial was quoted in the *Independent*: 'I said you could not have pig-ignorant peasants supervising classes, but you needed people of good education with appropriate training.' (Garner, 2001).

There is also concern from the practitioners themselves, as evidenced in Slater's (2004) article detailing teachers' views that claim an increase in time and work when working with support staff. The 'remodelling the workforce' agenda claims to help reduce teachers' workloads and improve standards in schools. But, of course, employing more teaching assistants will only reduce workloads for teachers if the benefits to be gained by their input are not outweighed for teachers by the extra management responsibility that comes from having another adult in one's classroom to direct. And this is not always the case.

Randall (2004), in her study of one school's approach to managing and developing support workers in classrooms, found little, if any, reduction in teachers' workloads. A more frightening scenario is conjectured by Wragg in his regular back-page column in the *The Times Educational Supplement* (9 January, 2004). In considering a spoof leaked DfES document, he reveals that the government is even considering a school without teachers. The leaked document outlined a plan for schools whereby headteachers would be the only qualified teachers employed. Somewhere along the continuum between spoof and duped is a danger that teachers' previous goodwill about workplace reform is being tested to the limit.

There is some confusion surrounding the role of support workers due to the fact that there are many different types of support workers with many different names giving rise to several nominalist fallacies. Some clarification can be discovered in the findings from a DfEE-funded research project (2000). The project investigated the management, role and training of learning support assistants and identified four areas of support: for pupils, for teachers, for the curriculum and for the school. The term 'teaching assistant' was employed in this good practice guide to signify a subtle change in role for some support staff. In order to make the best and most productive use of a growing number and types of support workers in the classroom, teachers need to have a source of advice and guidance in relation to the range of ways in which they can best collaborate with them. *Working with Support in the Classroom*, we hope, will provide such a source. It is hoped, in tune with O'Brien and Garner's (2001) feelings, to make visible the high-quality work undertaken by those who serve as support workers in schools. There has been little recognition in the past of the range of expertise support workers have been developing. No longer are they seen as doing purely menial jobs, such as washing the paint pots – although someone has to do that! The complex staffing structures being developed in most schools demand exceptional leadership and management skills to ensure everyone understands his or her own and others' roles and responsibilities, who to go to for advice and help, and how to access professional development opportunities.

In editing this book, we believed that, although there was a job to be done in offering support to teachers in deciding on the most productive ways of working alongside non-teaching adults in their classrooms, this was a job that would be better accomplished by gathering together a group of people who could each cast light on one part of the area, rather than entering into a make-believe world in which a couple of college professors pretend to have worthwhile expertise in the range of situations in which teachers and other significant adults work together with children in educational settings. So the book looks back at previous practices, but also towards the future as we make our way along the rocky road to 'remodelling the workforce'.

Our intended audience is primarily teachers and student teachers. However, we hope the book will also be of relevance if you are one of the 'significant others' to whom we are referring – if, for example, you are a teaching assistant, a nursery nurse or aspire to be an HLTA. You may even be a hybrid – both a teacher and a 'significant other' – if you are, for example, a qualified teacher who works in special needs or in a service that offers support to children for whom English is a second language.

The book covers early years settings in schools, and primary and secondary classrooms. It will be of special interest to those who work with children with special educational needs. It will, we hope, also be of interest to teaching assistants themselves as they develop their roles and relationships with those with whom they work in classrooms and schools. It is also hoped that student teachers and newly qualified teachers might find it useful as they begin to understand the complexities of schools as organizations and the importance of interpersonal skills and facilitative management strategies that are so important in the day-to-day running of schools.

In inviting contributors we were anxious to encourage them to adopt an easy and engaging writing style, and have done our best to ensure that they have done so. Our hope is that *Working with Support in the Classroom* will make easy and enjoyable reading, making general points about the topic through the careful selection of exemplars of good practice. Much of the time this has meant that authors have written in the first person, introducing stories from personal experience in the classroom. However, in order to make such stories effective, they are often used in order to support general points.

The content of the book is organized in a way that raises a range of issues, contexts and roles to be discussed from a number of perspectives. The following roles, contexts and issues will be represented at some point in the text, whether in individual chapters or in the joining narrative in this introduction. Particular roles that are discussed and illustrated in this book are those of the teaching assistant, learning support worker, learning mentor, nursery nurse, parent, teacher, student teacher, care assistant, community visitor, lunchtime organizer, pupil and headteacher. The contexts covered in this book range from those where the support of children with special educational needs is the main focus to those where the support of children with English as a second language is taking place; work in early years settings; work in primary and secondary classrooms; and work in the wider school environment, such as the playground. Some examples of Excellence in Cities and Education Action Zone projects, where learning mentors have been developed, are also illustrated in Chapters 4 and 10.

The book provides guidance for teachers who have responsibility for directing the work of teaching assistants and significant others in the classroom. It does so in a number of ways.

- An editorial overview in Chapter 11 draws attention to professional concerns (including ethical issues) in relation to the use of adults other than teachers in supporting pupils' learning.
- First-hand accounts of successful classroom practice show what works. These accounts have been written from a range of perspectives, including those of teaching assistants, classroom assistants, nursery nurses and others working alongside teachers, headteachers, parents and pupils.
- Various chapters discuss the development of effective collaborative practice between teachers and others in a range of contexts.

In *Working with Support in the Classroom* we want to explore and map the development of roles and functions of people other than qualified teachers in classrooms. The individual chapters provide stories of successful practice and ideas for improving collaborative work between teachers and significant others who work alongside teachers to support children's learning.

●●● Structure of the book

In this, the introductory chapter, we have presented a joining narrative that we hope helps to weave the individual contributions into a coherent whole. This narrative includes ideas for ways in which readers can develop their practice in relating to, and working with, other colleagues in the classroom. These ideas may be simple general statements or occasionally blinding flashes, inspirational moves and organizational tips. A number of the authors are publishing for the first time. The challenge to the editors has been to 'get inside' the chapters to make the book a coherent whole and to join up what appears to be a complex and challenging area of education as the government tries to reshape and remodel the workforce in schools.

Chapter 2 describes the role taken by a senior citizen volunteer in Ellington Primary School, Maidenhead. It focuses on how valuing diversity can support the development of a child's self-esteem. The author interviewed the community visitor, the headteacher, a nursery teacher and the children to enable her to write the story of the collaboration. Valuing diversity is hugely important, and this chapter looks at the ways in which the prejudices that are held by all children and adults develop and become embedded from an early age. A consideration of some ways in which we can tackle the problems of prejudice by including adults other than teachers in classrooms is presented.

Chapter 3 explores those support workers employed specifically to help children with special educational needs. This chapter poses questions about what we want from our special needs learning support assistants and examines the skills they need. It also questions what we are currently asking of them – for example, is it right that, at present, many learning support assistants are doing the majority of teaching of some children? The chapter also discusses different ways of using support, including in-class, group and individual support; group and individual withdrawal; and a number of different ways of conceiving the role of support assistant, including the support assistant as strolling player, repeat-play tape recorder and demonstrator, and as an interpreter, challenger and thought-provoker. The chapter explores practical ways of working together and considers the strengths and weaknesses of working in teams. The author believes that a well informed teaching assistant and a teacher who is willing to make the most of the partnership is a dynamic and effective team that can make inclusion a reality in the classroom and enhance the learning of all children.

Chapter 4 describes the role of a relatively new breed, the learning mentor. It outlines training for learning mentors and gives a perspective on the role of the learning mentor and his or her contribution to supporting children with specific needs that is beyond the scope of Chapter 3. It draws on examples of practice given by 'Matthew', a learning mentor from the first pilot project in primary schools in Merseyside. Through reading Matthew's story it is hoped you will get an insight into the day-to-day work of a learning mentor as he tackles the educational, social and emotional problems of the pupils in his care. Matthew provides an important male role model for pupils, and he has close connections with the local community, which gives him credibility and status with pupils, parents and teachers. He works as a school-based counsellor and as an advocate, ensuring vulnerable children are looked after and have someone as their 'champion'.

The focus of Chapter 5 is on the ways in which teachers and other adults, in supporting roles, can work together for the most effective learning in the classroom. Recent Ofsted and other reports about mathematics teaching suggest that learning is most effective when adults who support children are fully involved in planning and understand the learning objectives of the lesson. However, experience in working with such adults on training courses suggests that some teachers, particularly at Key Stages 2 and 3, are only recently becoming used to having other adults in the classroom. Training sessions with teachers confirm this view, and this suggests that there are many issues to resolve if working partnerships are to flourish. The chapter explores the qualities required of an adult working in a support role in mathematics lessons and the qualities required of the teacher in order to create effective working partnerships. The authors' experience of working with teaching assistants who support children learning mathematics leads them to believe that there are three crucial issues the classroom teacher must consider in order to ensure effective learning: communication, competence and confidence. All these can be developed through, and in turn strengthen, a good working relationship between the teacher and teaching assistant.

Chapter 6 looks at the different roles played in the classroom by adults other than teachers in addressing the ICT needs of pupils. In doing so it takes account of the classroom environment; programmes of study within the curriculum; the learning needs of individuals, and differences due to pupils' ages. It is argued that the teacher and classroom assistant should be able to create a good working environment for the children which embraces ICT in a natural way. A teaching assistant can also develop skills in ICT alongside children in activities if he or she is willing to see him or herself as a learner too. In the case of teaching assistants who are expert users of ICT, they will be invaluable in supporting the children in their learning. A teaching assistant could be very usefully employed working across the whole school with ICT, liaising closely with the ICT co-ordinator. The assistant who is designated to a class is also discussed in this chapter.

There is also some exploration of the scope for the classroom assistant to contribute to the preparation of materials when children wish to present their ideas. A consideration of the role of ICT in professional development is given and its use in collaborating in the production of materials, either for other staff in the school, outside agencies (including the LEA and Ofsted) or for communicating with parents and governors. The chapter also details many practical strategies and tools for collaborative work between teachers, teaching assistants and pupils.

The next chapter, Chapter 7, leads us into a story of why teachers and nursery nurses need to work well together. The reason for using the now discarded term 'nursery nurse' is that the author researched this role recently before the changes took effect as a result of workforce reform legislation, and she wished to document and recognize the valuable role played in the past by those termed nursery nurses. This role has not been lost to the profession as yet, which has merely changed the name to teaching assistant to fit in with the government's workforce remodelling initiative.

The chapter outlines the advantages of establishing a high-quality relationship between teachers and support workers and discusses the disadvantages of failing to do so. It sketches the characters of a newly qualified teacher and an experienced nursery nurse in the form of a dialogue. The conversation begins at the start of the day and then hopes to capture key moments of the day when interactions that depict wariness, attempts to develop teamwork, role conflicts, shared humour and different approaches to working with children occur. The dialogue continues over a few weeks to capture the ups and downs of a relationship between a teacher and nursery nurse. Conclusions are then drawn about the need for effective working partnerships, and the author discusses the training needs of nursery nurses. Finally, some features of effective partnership practice are identified and discussed.

The approach in Chapter 8 aims to provide teachers with further insight into the practical implications of working with students as assistants in classroom settings. The authors (themselves recently classrooms teachers and now tutors in higher education) look at issues raised with reference to current partnerships in initial teacher training and their own practical experience. Case stories are used to highlight problematic, practical issues experienced by teachers. Examples of good practice in coaching students are presented throughout the chapter, using a variety of methods to communicate ideas. The focus on communication covers such issues as informal discussions, clarifying tasks, honesty in feedback and dealing with difficulties. The section dealing with expectations includes an apprenticeship model of learning to teach in school; target setting and setting realistic goals; and strategies to deal with mistakes. This chapter presents a refreshing perspective from two recent recruits from schools to higher education.

Chapter 9 is based on interviews and discussions with staff from a variety of backgrounds, e.g. learning mentors, bilingual assistants, lunchtime organizers, and teachers and parents from Temple Primary School in north Manchester, where the author is a governor. The voices of the children – the recipients of the support and teaching – are also documented from group interviews with a range of children aged 6 to 11 years. The chapter tells the story of the challenges and dilemmas of working in and managing a large primary school with a varied staff, in an area where there is a rich variety of ethnic groups. The title of the chapter

('All different, all equal') is also the school motto, one that is adequately evidenced in the responses from staff and pupils in the interviews that form the basis of this chapter. Children in the later years of the primary school demonstrate their understanding of the different roles of adults in a sophisticated way and give food for thought about ways in which we can support them in their 'lived experiences' of school life. The concluding section addresses what messages can be learned from talking to the children and adults who inhabit the school.

In Chapter 10, the government's workforce remodelling initiative is examined through the eyes of two headteachers who have been seconded to their LEAs. In the case of Angela, the brief was to manage and implement the workforce remodelling and, for Barbara, to investigate what headteachers and schools think about the initiative. The voices of these two headteachers were sought through informal interviews, and a great deal of information about the workforce remodelling initiative can be learned, not least the problems of defining roles and developing job descriptions for a wide range of support workers. The various different roles, as described in some of the preceding chapters, are complex and subject to influences of school context, needs and the personalities of both those who are support workers and those who manage them.

In the final chapter the author identifies and discusses key issues and features from the previous chapters in the book. She provides guidance and support for developing successful practice in collaborative work with, support assistants, learning mentors, members of the community, parents, nursery nurses, students, teaching assistants and special needs assistants. She draws conclusions and highlights and discusses important issues concerning working together in classrooms; role definition and description; support for curriculum subjects; and professional development and training. This chapter hopes to bring together a set of practices that support collaborative work in schools. As this book was being completed there were still a great many changes being implemented in the remodelling of the workforce. The future is uncertain, and some of the main players in the field (the unions representing teachers and teaching assistants) are trying to 'peer into the future' and are waiting to make their next move. This could well be to withdraw from the agreement because there is little financial support for schools and a lack of good pay and work conditions for the new breed of teaching assistant. Let us hope that these difficult issues can be resolved and that teachers and support workers can make the vision a reality.

●●● References

DfEE (2000) *Working with Teaching Assistants: A Good Practice Guide*. London: DfEE Publications.

DfES (2002) *Developing the Role of School Support Staff: The Consultation*. London: DfES Publications.

Garner, R. (2001) 'Teaching union leader apologises for "pig ignorant" remark', *Independent*, 17 November.

O'Brien, T. and Garner, P. (2001) *Untold Stories: Learning Support Assistants and their Work*. Stoke-on-Trent: Trentham Books.

Randall, H. (2004) 'An investigation into some strategies for enhancing the role of teaching assistants in a Liverpool primary school.' Unpublished MSc dissertation, Liverpool Hope University College, Liverpool.

Slater, J. (2004) 'Workload: teachers speak out', *The Times Educational Supplement*, 9 January.

Wragg, E.C. (2004) Weekly column in *The Times Educational Supplement*, 9 January.

●●● Chapter 2

Valuing diversity: the role of support workers in the early years

Wendy Bignold

A child's self-esteem is crucial to his or her sense of self. Developing a sense of self is intricately linked with developing a sense of others, of individuals and of groups. This is particularly important in young children as they are beginning to make sense of the world around them and the community of which they are a part. In today's Britain children are growing up in an increasingly diverse society and valuing diversity is an important role for schools.

There are many definitions of what education should be and for what it should prepare children. A common philosophy is that promoted by Dowling (2000): 'The confident person is equipped to deal with life, whether in school or work or social situations.' Such a philosophy does not simply see children as '"adults in waiting"' but as people, 'social beings who are trying to participate in and make sense of their world – whatever their age' (David, 1998: 25). With young children, their own confidence and self-esteem are key influences on their understanding of the world they are in, an understanding based on their perceptions of themselves, of those around them and of how those around them respond to them.

Children begin to 'identify' themselves from birth onwards, building a picture based on other people's responses to them. In the early stages of development this is based on key people, such as parents, carers and siblings. Because of their immaturity young children are easily influenced by the views and opinions of those around them. As children get older other people become influential as children begin to interact with a wider range of people, and others such as teachers and support workers in school and non-school settings. Young children show considerable interest in what people do, especially people who are significant to them. They tune into how other people react to different situations and these become a reference point for their own behaviour. This chapter is concerned with how children develop prejudices and stereotypes about certain groups of people and how they can be encouraged to value diversity by interacting with significant others in the role of support workers.

Prejudice is forming an opinion about a person with little or no information or evidence on which to base that opinion. It means that a person is prejudged by others, perhaps even before they have met. Prejudices tend to be aimed at easily identifiable groups of people based on stereotypical views of that group. There are many reasons for people developing stereotypes of others, which are complex and varied. Stereotypes are based on people's personal experiences or interactions with members of certain groups. The experience may only be with one person. However, other identifiable members of the same group may quickly be judged on the individual's actions. The media have a key role to play in both reinforcing and combating stereotypes. A good example of this is gender-biased adverts which are played during children's television programmes. Boys are often seen playing violent games with action figures while girls are more likely to be shown caring for baby dolls. This may be an extreme example but it is one which everyone is familiar with. Such adverts reinforce children's stereotypes of what is appropriate gender behaviour.

While stereotypes can be harmless they can reduce people's opportunities in life, and negative stereotypes can easily become prejudices against groups of people. Prejudices are passed from generation to generation, often in subtle and unrecognized ways. When prejudiced attitudes are expressed, discrimination occurs. It is therefore important to encourage young children to value diversity as a way of overcoming stereotypes and so prejudices. This can be successfully done in a non-overt way in the early years before prejudices are too firmly established. With older children it may be necessary to challenge prejudices more directly.

Support workers in schools have a key role to play here and so do teachers in the ways that they interact with them. If support workers are used in schools then teachers are always role models to their pupils on how to interact with such individuals and groups. Support workers can be used in stereotypical ways to further children's knowledge and understanding of different areas of the curriculum but they can also be used in non-stereotypical ways to encourage children to value diversity and to overcome stereotypical views. An example of this would be a school which invites a person in a wheelchair in to talk about being in a wheelchair or his or her disability. This would be using the person in a stereotypical or traditional way which may be of benefit to children's ability to empathize with others. Much more effective, though, would be inviting such a person in to hear children read or to help a group of children with a numeracy activity on a regular basis. The perceived disability is irrelevant in this situation. The children see the 'helper' as someone who can help them with their work. The interaction that is likely to take place will be one to one, e.g. hearing a reader or working with a small group on a numeracy problem. This provides the children with an opportunity to interact with the individual and to get to know him or her. They may ask questions about the wheelchair as children are often intrigued by obvious differences but, as their relationships with the 'helper' are developed, they will come to recognize the different things that this person does with them and the wheelchair will become less and less important. The teacher is crucial here, both as a positive role model in his or her relationship with the 'helper' and in enabling the children to see the 'helper' as an individual with many different talents.

One school which is successfully using support workers in non-stereotypical ways is Ellington Primary and Nursery School, Maidenhead. A small school, it has recently been praised by Ofsted for its approach to pupils' personal development: 'The school's care, guidance and provision for pupils' personal development are very good' (2003).

Ellington School is a smaller than average primary with approximately 140 pupils on roll. Almost all pupils come from the same local area which is a mix of local authority and owner-occupied housing. Thirty-three percent of pupils are entitled to free school meals. Eighty-four percent are from minority ethnic groups, mainly Pakistani, and speak English as an additional language. Many children live in an extended family unit, sharing their homes with grandparents, aunts and uncles and sometimes cousins. Other cultural backgrounds include recently arrived refugees and travellers. Forty-two percent of the children are on the school's register of special educational needs, which is higher than the national average percentage. Sixteen pupils have a statement of special needs, which is significantly higher than the national average (Ofsted, 2003). Given this profile of the pupil population, many educationalists would describe the school as 'challenging'. While this may be so it is a challenge which headteacher, Rehana Juna and her staff are meeting: 'Ellington is a good school with very good and excellent features. The pupils achieve well because the teaching is good with a significant proportion that is very good and at times excellent' (Ofsted, 2003). The school has been commended by Ofsted for being fully inclusive and ensuring that all pupils have equal opportunities. This inclusivity is underpinned by the positive way in which support workers are used. They, along with all staff, 'present positive role models to the children' (Mission

Statement, 2001). By examining the contributions of one support worker at Ellington, the good practice which the school has developed in this area can be illustrated.

Derek is a member of the surrounding community. As a septuagenarian he was looking for a local interest which would make good use of his life skills and expertise in his retirement. Describing himself as an experienced father and, more recently, an experienced grandfather volunteering to help at a local school was an obvious choice for him: 'I have always been involved in the community and see my role at Ellington as part of this. I am happy contributing [to the community] in this way because of my love for small children which relates to my role as a grandfather.'

Derek's role as a support worker in the Nursery class clearly has a twofold benefit. First, and most significantly, is the positive effect it has on the young children. Derek makes a regular, weekly visit to the Nursery class and spends an hour and a half with the children. The nursery teacher, Jill Pockett, encourages him to get fully involved in whatever is going on. On any one visit he can find himself doing a number of different things, such as:

- Setting up outdoor equipment.
- Playing football or other outdoor games.
- Being a friend to an individual child or a group of children.
- Assisting with supervision of outdoor play and routines.
- Playing with the trains on the floor inside.
- Making playdough models with groups of children.
- Playing simple games with individuals on the computer.
- Preparing the morning snack, serving it and helping the children to eat it.
- Reading stories to small groups and individuals.
- Modelling social skills.

During a regular 90-minute visit he may accomplish a wide range of activities with the children, as shown above. They see him taking on different activities and carrying out different tasks which may not be stereotypical for someone of his age group, playing football or lying on the floor pushing trains around, or for someone of his gender, preparing and serving food. The variety of activities that he is involved with and the nature of each of them are highly significant for this reason. Depending on the extent to which the teacher discusses his role with the children they will, consciously or subconsciously, see him engaged in a range of activities, some of which will be different from expectations of him based on his age and gender. This provides an opportunity to challenge children's early stereotypes of certain groups of people, again either consciously or subconsciously. Spontaneous opportunities for furthering children's personal development can often arise and teachers need to make good use of unplanned, as well as planned, opportunities to maximize on their learning potential. The importance of this is discussed by Hayes, who offers advice to teachers which could clearly relate to this case study:

> *Opportunities for [personal] development exist within the planned and unplanned curriculum. Sometimes an older pupil's spontaneous question can provide the basis for powerful discussions and provocative debate. Younger pupils can ask questions and make statements that are profoundly simplistic, thereby causing a lot of soul searching about fundamental truths. It is important to be as honest as possible, including acknowledging when you are uncertain, but be careful not to become trapped in conversations which are slightly unwholesome or unduly controversial (1999: 19).*

Nursery teacher, Jill, identifies a range of benefits for the children from Derek's involvement with them. These relate either to him as a male role model or as an elder member of the community. He is also a 'white' role model:

> *Some of our fathers [her pupils' fathers] are shift workers or have driving jobs so the children do not always see their fathers in the evening or at weekends. It is important then that they have regular interaction with a man in their own nursery setting and see him involved in a wide range of tasks.*

Jill describes a lot of the younger girls as shy or very shy because of the cultural tendency for them naturally to defer to the boys in the Nursery. All the children have got to know and trust Derek through his regular, weekly contact with them. Jill recognizes that he has an awareness of when children need help and that he is very good at targeting the quieter, more reticent children to sit next to at snack time for a 'little chat'. All the staff at Ellington Nursery are female, apart from the site controller who does not have a significant amount of interaction with the Nursery children. This is a particularly important factor in the involvement of a male support worker, which Jill emphasizes: 'It is also great for the children to see Derek working alongside the three female nursery staff and to be the assistant rather than the "boss".'

Derek's involvement with the children as a septuagenarian enables them to see an older person in a variety of roles which they would not normally expect. When asked 'What do old people do?', the Nursery children gave some interesting and, as may be expected of children so young, rather stereotypical answers:

Old people sleep.
Tariq's grand-dad goes to the mosque but his grandma says he shouldn't because he is too old to go out.
Old people eat and sleep. They go outside for a walk.
Gardening.
Sitting down.
Walk with sticks.

This rather limited range of activities with which the children identify older people is quite a contrast to the range of activities that Jill encourages Derek to take on. This clearly demonstrates how, through planned and unplanned interaction, these children are experiencing something more diverse than is usual to them.

It is important not to deny Derek's age or experience and his related position in society if he is to feel valued as an individual. He himself sees his relationship with the children as one based on 'a grandfatherly attitude towards them all'. They show an awareness of his age, not in years but in relation to other people they know. One child commented: 'You haven't got any hair, Mr Bignold. My grand-dad hasn't got any hair either!' Elderly members of society are often portrayed in today's media as being less empowered than many younger groups of people, of being less active and having less to contribute to the community. It is important, therefore, that the children recognize Derek's age 'status' in order that they can be helped to recognize the prejudices which they will already be developing about such people. Jill recognizes that most of the children in the nursery class live in an extended family and so are living with their grandparents. This is a common tradition in Asian households from which most of the pupils at Ellington come. They are used to being around older people and are familiar with the sorts of roles they perform in the home and the community. Considerable research by the author on the Indian subcontinent and with Pakistani communities in the UK does show that older members of such households do generally conform to traditional gender and age-expected roles. A simple illustration of this would be for grandmothers to assist with the care of children and domestic duties while grandfathers would be less directly involved in these but may adopt more prominent roles outside the family, perhaps focused around places of worship. It is acknowledged that this is a simplistic generalization but one which has been found to be largely true (Bignold, 1994), although of course there will be exceptions to it. Given that most of the children are familiar with the traditional age and gender roles associated with grand-parents, it is particularly important that they interact with Derek in a variety of different situations as a means of acknowledging diversity among men and older groups of people. Although Derek's ethnic background is not important to the school headteacher, Rehana does see his involvement with Ellington as a member of the original white community as being a positive signal to those inside and outside the school.

It is important that teachers have identified their own prejudices and stereo-types in order that they recognize them and then acknowledge the possibility of influencing their pupils with them. Once they have identified them teachers can plan appropriate activities or the use of support workers to ensure that children do not adopt these themselves. The importance of this process is emphasized by Siraj-Blatchford: 'Early childhood educators need to examine their own atti-tudes and prejudices and learn to deal with them in positive ways.' (2001: 105). One example of this happening is with trainee early years teachers at Liverpool Hope University College who are required to identify and consider their own prejudices and stereotypes in a module entitled 'Valuing diversity: the child, family and society'. They are encouraged to look for the roots of any negative prejudices that they hold and consider with their peers ways of overcoming these. Students always comment that, although they find the whole process dif-ficult and at times personally challenging, by the end of the course they are able to recognize both their own personal development and their professional devel-opment as early years practitioners. Only when the students have acknowledged their own prejudices can they support young children in overcoming theirs through a planned, and unplanned, curriculum. The role of support workers, as discussed in this case study, is one strategy that the students explore in relation to class, race, gender, age, religion, disability and sexuality. Trainee teachers are often unsure how to introduce diversity into an early years curriculum without being tokenistic. Support workers can be used effectively here in the type of role discussed earlier – for example, asking a woman of Indian origin to come in on one occasion to show the children how to wear a sari. A more meaningful learn-ing experience for the children would be to involve this person as a support worker if willing and on one of her visits to ask her to demonstrate how to wear saris and perhaps help some of the children dress up in them.

The teacher's own attitude to the potential of support workers in relation to valuing diversity is crucial as he or she acts as a role model to the children. Again, Hayes reminds newly qualified teachers of this: 'Your life and conduct provides the single most significant influence for the pupils in their school experience.' (1999: 18). This is particularly true of teachers of young children who are less influenced by their peers than older pupils and for whom significant adults, such as teachers, have a huge impact. Nursery teacher Jill clearly values Derek's contribution, as demonstrated by her encouragement for him to be fully involved in her class. As a result of this Derek feels that he is 'a totally integrated part of the nursery team – certainly not just a visitor. I have a positive relationship with the nursery teacher who sees me as an asset.' If this is how the nursery staff view him then it is more likely that the children will see him in a similarly positive light.

If any support worker is going to have a positive impact on the pupils that he or she works with then the pupils must enjoy the interaction. Clearly the Nursery children at Ellington enjoy Derek's weekly visits: 'They hear my footsteps coming up the corridor. When I come in they rush to greet me. Two particular boys, one white, one Asian, will run the length of the classroom and throw their arms around me!'

The second benefit of Derek's role as a support worker in the nursery is that it gives him a great amount of satisfaction as he experiences the warmth and affection he receives from staff and pupils. An unexpected outcome for him is that he now feels more relaxed with Asian adults and children. He recognizes that he now talks to Asian parents more confidently and more readily than he would previously have done. This is a good example of the process of lifelong learning and is really quite significant for somebody of his generation living in a town which was for many, many years, all white but which now has an increasingly multi-ethnic make-up: 'Being part of such a multicultural school and working with such a large proportion of ethnic minority children in Nursery I feel I contribute to their families being a part of British society.'

The potential of using support workers to promote diversity in non-traditional roles as discussed in this case study is not to discourage schools from using them in traditional roles too. It is to encourage teachers to look more widely at the potential of such adults in different areas of the curriculum. Derek does give an annual talk to Reception, Year 1 and Year 2 about what it was like to visit the seaside when he was a child. This is an obvious role for a child's grandparent or other older member of the community to be asked to fulfil. Using such first-hand sources in history topics is an excellent way of developing children's learning. It is particularly important in helping young children develop a sense of time and change over time and has been much documented by historians such as Claire (1996) Fines and Nichol (1997) and Hughes *et al.* (2000). One advantage of using visitors or volunteers in a traditional role in relation to valuing diversity is that it may be the first step in involving them in the school. People may be more likely to agree to come in for one session rather than to make a regular commitment. However, if they are warmly welcomed, made to feel valued and enjoy the interaction with the children, they are more likely to consider coming back. If they are initially invited in to talk about their own experiences or something which is very familiar to them then they will feel confident and clear about the expectations of them. Asking someone to come in and play with the children or assist a group with a numeracy activity may be quite daunting because of a potential lack of clarity over what is expected of them and what exactly they will be asked to do. This first-step approach may be something that a school should consider if planning to increase its number of volunteer support workers.

Any school which is hoping to attract volunteer support workers as a means of valuing diversity needs to give careful consideration to how it can welcome them and value them, both initially and in the long term. Ellington has clearly been successful in doing this by the ambience that has been created in the entrance area and reinforced throughout the school:

> *Our community ethos is a significant part of our strength and we endeavour to ensure that all within the school are valued for their personal skills and the contribution they make. This is regardless of race, culture, religion, gender, age, or disability. All school policies contain a statement on equal opportunities and there are frequent reviews of resources to ensure they contain no discriminatory material (School Prospectus, 2003).*

As a visitor to the school Derek describes it as being very welcoming and very calm: 'The displays in the public areas and throughout the school have a strong emphasis on equality and how people should value one another. This carries over into the classrooms in a big way.'

Clearly it is important for any visitors (and especially regular visitors) to feel valued for who they are as individuals. An obvious way of developing a welcoming ethos is through the effective use of displays in common areas which have obviously had an impact in this case study.

●●● Initial considerations for schools

The following are some initial considerations for schools wanting to use support workers:

- First impressions of the school and its ethos, as discussed above.
- The ways in which visitors are greeted.
- The physical layout of the buildings and the ease of access through appropriate signage or physical access, for example.
- The local reputation of the school which the school can have a positive influence on by working with the local media.

In making a long-term commitment to a school, an individual may be giving a significant amount of his or her own time over the course of a year or a number of years. Derek has made this commitment because of the personal enjoyment and satisfaction he receives from his regular contact with the children. Alongside this, he has been made to feel an important member of the school community by the headteacher and other staff. His role has developed and he is Foundation Stage governor and vice-chair of the governing body. He feels intricately involved in the school through his weekly visits to the Nursery and he feels fully valued by the staff who always make time to talk to him and who welcome him into the staffroom at playtimes. Although his main role is with the Nursery class he does have contact with other age groups and with the whole school at the encouragement of the headteacher. He has fulfilled traditional roles in the school for which support workers can be a very useful resource, such as presenting certificates in assemblies or supporting individual children with special needs at SATs time:

> *I have a closer relationship with the younger children by virtue of my role in the Nursery and the frequency of my visits. When it comes to SATs time I help some of Years 5 and 6 with their reading of the questions. It's a different kind of relationship and involvement which is not so close but which I enjoy and feel that I can help the children with.*

The nature of such involvement is very different from that in the Nursery but is an important one for valuing him in a number of different roles and recognizing him as being able to make a range of contributions. This is a further example of how the school refuses to fit him into one stereotypical mould. The headteacher's effective use of him in different roles further reinforces his individuality, his skills and expertise to the pupils.

●●● Long-term considerations for schools

'Special guests'

This includes staff and governors' attitudes towards volunteers as support workers – for example, are they welcoming, and do they all recognize the potential benefit to the children's learning? All staff and governors need to be committed to the involvement of volunteer support workers to ensure that no negative messages are conveyed to the pupils that may combat the effective use of these adults in the children's personal development. Schools may want to hold whole-staff training sessions to ensure that there is a common view. For example, being invited to assemblies as 'special guests' would demonstrate acceptance into the school community. Schools may need to consider flexible timing of assemblies in order to accommodate the 'special guests'. It must be acknowledged that many adults, particularly those working in schools in a voluntary capacity, have other commitments during their day and so may not be able to attend on different occasions.

Strategies and facilities

These include strategies for dealing with negative comments and behaviour from pupils or staff towards support workers – for example, are clear strategies in place, perhaps in the form of a school policy, for dealing with incidents such as racist name-calling to volunteers? All schools are required to have an equal opportunities policy and an anti-racist policy and clear strategies for dealing with negative behaviour in relation to this. Schools will want to ensure that this does not only focus on supporting and protecting pupils but also on adults in the school community.

Are general facilities available to support workers – for example, are they welcomed into the staffroom for a coffee? Ninety minutes interaction with young children can be very tiring for some people. Is there a quiet place where they can have a drink and a rest before they leave? Teachers who have support workers in their classrooms should make sure that these adults are clear on what facilities are available to them while they are in school. Inviting them into the staffroom generally creates an atmosphere of trust and mutual support, although there may be issues of confidentiality of information and so all staff need to be aware of other adults sharing their facilities to ensure that no one is compromised. Are there specific facilities, for example, if a support worker has a mobility issue can he or she move freely around the school, or will he or she need some assistance and who will provide this? Schools may need to provide car-parking facilities close to the entrance. An older pupil or adult may be needed to act as a translator for a support worker to communicate with the children or the teacher if they do not share a common language.

Appropriate roles

Are the tasks the individual support worker is being expected to take on reasonable in relation to his or her age, culture or experience? This requires the teacher to find out something about the support worker and his or her skills and interests then planning activities to maximize on these. This has the added benefit of making the adult feel valued. Does the individual understand what is expected of him or her in relation to valuing diversity? Is there an opportunity to discuss this with the teacher? Teachers need to ensure that there is effective communication between themselves and other adults supporting them in the classroom. Time has to be planned for this and so the teacher may invite the adult in for a visit prior to his or her first session when the teacher is free to talk with the support worker.

Criminal Records Bureau

Is it necessary for the support worker to undergo a Criminal Records Bureau check? How will the school support him or her in this in relation to the cost or his or her understanding of the process and its necessity? Might it be seen as disrespectful to the individual to require him or her to undergo the check? What will happen if a criminal record is disclosed? How will this be handled sensitively? Schools need to consider these issues and have a clear policy on who requires disclosures and how the process will be managed.

Dealing with difficult issues

What would happen if the individual made a sexist comment or other inappropriate remark to a pupil or member of staff? When schools invite new volunteers in, it may not be possible for the headteacher or teacher involved to make a full and accurate assessment of the individual's own attitudes towards other groups of people. How might any potential risk here be lessened and how would any issues be dealt with? Does the individual need any guidance at the beginning to make clear the school's ethos or commitment to equal opportunities? The head-teacher has a key role to play here. He or she may choose to give a new support worker a tour of the school during which time the ethos and commitment to equal opportunities can be verbally emphasized, while its physical influence may be pointed out in displays and so on. This provides an opportunity for both parties to ask questions and, ultimately, for the support worker to decide that he or she would not fit in with the school's philosophy. If the headteacher has concerns about the visitor not supporting the school's philosophy this would need to be raised very sensitively and a solution sought. One solution may be to use the support worker in a very different role from the one discussed in this chapter, possibly where he or she assists with administration but does not have a significant amount of interaction with the pupils. Maintaining the school library would be an example of a different role someone in this position could take on.

The early years are a crucial time for children to learn about themselves and other people around them, in their family, their community and the wider world. In order for this to happen effectively Siraj-Blatchford and Clarke (2000; cited in Siraj-Blatchford, 2001) identified 13 elements that should be included in an effective early years curriculum. Eight of these have been illustrated by this case study where the curriculum:

- Fosters children's self-esteem
- Acknowledges the cultural and linguistic backgrounds of all children
- Values what boys and girls can do equally [or men and women as in this example]
- Fosters an awareness of diversity in class, gender, ability and culture
- Promotes respect for similarity and difference
- Challenges bias and prejudice
- Promotes principles of inclusion and equity
- Supports the participation of the parents in the children's learning [and other family members] (Siraj-Blatchford and Clarke, 2000, cited in Siraj-Blatchford, 2001)

Ofsted commended Ellington for its involvement of parents and community members in children's learning: 'The initiatives to involve parents in the life of the school and the contribution of the community to pupil's learning are excellent' (2003). This case study has demonstrated one effective way of using volunteer support workers in non-traditional roles. For any school in today's multi-ethnic society the valuing of diversity is crucial and the overcoming of prejudices and stereotypes is a key aspect of this. Ellington Primary and Nursery School has successfully taken on this challenge and its achievements are rightly being recognized alongside the important contribution that support workers have to make in this.

●●● References

Bignold, W. (1994) 'Educational provision and access for girls in Chitral Valley, Pakistan.' MA dissertation, University of Reading.

Claire, H. (1996) *Reclaiming Our Pasts – Equality and Diversity in the Primary History Curriculum.* Stoke-on-Trent: Trentham Books.

David, T. (1998) 'Changing minds: young children and society,' in L. Abbott and H. Pugh (eds) *Training to Work in the Early Years.* Buckingham: Open University Press.

Dowling, M. (2000) *Young Children's Personal, Social and Emotional Development.* London: Paul Chapman Publishers.

Ellington Primary and Nursery School (2001) *Mission Statement.*

Ellington Primary and Nursery School (2003) *Ellington Primary School Prospectus.*

Fines, J. and Nichol, J. (1997) *Teaching Primary History.* London: Heinemann.

Hayes, D. (1999) *Planning, Teaching and Class Management in Primary Schools.* London: David Fulton.

Hughes, P., Cox, K., Goddard, G. (2000) *Primary History Curriculum Guide.* London: David Fulton.

Ofsted (2003) *Summary of the Inspection Report: Ellington Primary School.* London: Ofsted.

Siraj-Blatchford, I. (2001) 'Diversity and learning in the early years,' in G. Pugh (ed.) *Contemporary Issues in the Early Years – Working Collaboratively for Children* (3rd edn). London: Paul Chapman Publishing.

Chapter 3

Making the most of the teaching assistant for special educational needs

Wendy Hall

Introduction

Whether you welcome teaching assistants with open arms or accept them with some trepidation, teaching assistants are part of the future of education. The teaching assistants can be the greatest asset some teachers will ever have, other than winning the lottery – a less likely event – or, for some, as reported in the *Guardian* (25 April 2002), the teaching assistant can be viewed as extra work and responsibility that is not needed. Ofsted (cited by Curtis, 2002) also found that, while the quality of teaching may improve with teaching assistants, the workload may also increase and not decrease. The findings of the National Evaluation Project (Wilson *et al.*, 2003), however, reported positively on the benefits versus the burdens of working with teaching assistants. The aims of this evaluation project, cited by the Scottish Council for Research in Education (SCRE) (2001), were to:

- identify examples of effective practice;
- explore management implications for teaching assistants;
- document training requirements;
- record and assess unexpected outcomes;
- identify problems.

The main findings (Wilson *et al.*, 2003) indicated that, of teaching assistants in the survey sample, 60 per cent spent more time engaged in group or individual teaching. They also had high expectations of pupils and this had a direct impact on pupil attainment.

The purpose of this chapter is to suggest ways in which a busy classroom teacher can make the best of the teaching assistant who supports special needs children. The National Association for Special Educational Needs (NASEN) (2002) provides further valuable guidance for schools and LEAs in the form of policy documents that provide advice on the role of schools and governors, LEA responsibility and the role of central government.

I will address the different roles assigned to the teaching assistant, including that of the learning support assistant. Some authorities and schools have quite clear delineation between learning support assistants and teaching assistants while others only appoint teaching assistants who undertake the work of all these roles. I will use the term teaching assistant throughout but may cover aspects of a variety of roles of the support worker.

There is some disquiet about teaching assistants as a result of government initiatives which have suggested that teaching assistants may replace classroom teachers in the teaching role, as reported by Woodward and Smithers in the *Guardian* (17 Spetember 2002), or as identified by the NUT (cited by Mercer, 2002), as an attempt to cover teacher shortages with teaching assistants or even to support inclusive practice by the use of teaching assistants; rather than specialist teachers. I do not intend to engage in a political debate about the reasons behind the use of teaching assistants, rather I wish to address the issue that, given the government's commitment to increasing their numbers by an extra 50,000 by 2006 (cited by Smithers – *Guardian*, 18 October 2002), teaching assistants are a resource to be used and we need to decide how best they might be trained, managed and supported in assisting the children and teacher.

●●● How are these teaching assistants different from previous assistants?

Classroom help has been around for years and has, to a certain extent, always caused some controversy. Regular help in a classroom is not a new concept. However, the way that the help fits together with the role of the teacher is rapidly changing. The concept of the role of the teacher is changing and the formalization of the role of the teaching assistant is causing ripples in staffrooms.

Previously, enthusiastic parents provided help in the classroom, some of whom could spare a few hours each week to assist the teacher. There were many different practices even within the same school. Some teachers welcomed a parent, while others preferred to keep their classrooms to themselves. These parents were largely unpaid and to a certain degree felt little obligation to the school. Sometimes they could be unreliable when a priority outside school demanded their time. They could withdraw their help at short notice and until relatively recently they were not checked against police records. Over the last 15 years there has been a subtle shift to make these arrangements more formal, first by requiring police clearance, then by advertising for paid posts in recognition of the work undertaken. Classroom assistants' contribution was formalized and it was recognized as a job within the school. They were expected to turn up regularly at certain times and not to take time off. There was to be a commitment to the school. Classroom assistants became more like lunchtime supervisors in their work contracts and the numbers increased. Revell (*Guardian*, 23 October 2002) quoted figures which reveal that in the year up to October 2002, non-teaching staff numbers rose by 15 per cent in English schools. NFER research in 2002 (cited at www.literacytrust.org.uk/database/teachassistant.html) found that 'they are now widely regarded in schools as valuable members of staff'. The present move to recruit more support in classrooms is a significant one as it is government initiated and changes how teachers work. Clare in the *Telegraph* (23 October 2002) reported Estelle Morris as claiming this to be part of a 'pedagogy fit for the 21st century'. She hoped that teachers would be freed of 'unnecessary burdens', and be allowed to concentrate on 'higher order' teaching. She likened teachers to consultant surgeons. The notion behind Estelle Morris's proposals was that the new band of teaching assistants would not just be an extra pair of hands but would fundamentally change how teachers work, how they conceive of their role, giving them a more strategic role in terms of planning and managing learning. This move also attempted to recognize that it does not always have to be the teacher who supervises the majority of the class – it could be the teaching assistant who supervises the majority of the class, which would be undertaking work set by the teacher while the teacher has a sustained and focused teaching input with a particular group, or the teaching assistant may undertake this focused work under the guidance of the teacher. This, however, was strongly opposed by the teachers' unions. One worry was that this could then be extended to supervising classes while teachers are away on courses or absent through illness and so, consequently, reduce the use of supply teachers. This has to be a matter of the headteacher's conscience as, in many instances, the use of the regular, well trained and informed teaching assistant may be a better option than a series of supply teachers who lack continuity and knowledge of the children and who do little more than childmind. This should be an option that headteachers have – that, in the absence of a suitable supply teacher and in the presence of a good teaching assistant for short periods of time, the teaching assistant could take the class under the supervision of another teacher.

●●● Teacher support or child support?

What is the role of the teaching assistant? Different LEAs have a variety of job descriptions relating to the role of the teaching assistant, and schools will need to work within the role designated in the school in which they reside and within the emerging National Framework. However, the BBC's education web page, in an article entitled 'What are teaching assistants?' (2001), described teaching assistants as 'people who support fully qualified teachers, taking on non teaching tasks such as photocopying, but also with duties such as listening to children read'. DfES (2000) guidance lists teaching assistants as support for the pupil, the teacher, the curriculum and the school.

Kerry (2002) details how, in Leicestershire, teaching assistants are used as learning mentors whom the pupils really value as they like having recourse to an adult who is neither parent nor teacher. It depends on how your authority/school and teacher view the role of the teaching assistant as to how the teaching assistant will be used. You may decide to use the teaching assistant as a general assistant undertaking non-teaching duties or you may decide the real value is in asking your teaching assistant to take on a similar role to the teacher, working with small groups of children with special educational needs. A pilot project in Scotland found that a number of teachers were uncertain about the best balance between using the teaching assistant on teaching or non-teaching tasks and, in some instances, this caused dissatisfaction when a teaching assistant was asked to undertake work he or she was less happy with (Wilson *et al.*, 2003). Each role has definite skills attached to it and requires different management and training. This chapter will focus on the role of the teaching assistant in supporting special needs children (whether this is direct teaching or supporting the teaching), as this is a growing area of concern.

An assistant who is largely used for classroom tasks will mostly not need to know about differentiation, motivation of children and management of tasks. He or she will, however, if used to the best advantage, need a schedule of work and tasks to be ongoing which may place a responsibility on the teacher to be organized, well planned and prepared well ahead of time in order for the assistant to be of any use. Indeed, Curtis (2002) reports that Ofsted found that, although teaching assistants enhanced the teaching, they did little to cut the workload of teachers and in some classrooms increased it because of this factor. An assistant who is used directly to support children engaged in work will require briefing about the task, will need a certain amount of training in inter-personal skills, in how children learn, in motivation and how to manage and differentiate tasks in order to provide the best for the children in the group. This in itself means the teacher has to take time to sit down with the assistant prior to setting tasks and to explain the learning outcomes, the focus of the task, the method used and how to differentiate should the need arise. The assistant will need to be sensitive to the personal needs of children needing extra support.

⬤⬤⬤ The role of the teaching assistant who works with children with SEN

What is the purpose of the teaching assistant? Teaching assistants were essentially introduced to raise the standard of achievement of children in schools, not neces-sarily to alleviate the workload of teachers. This latter concept has only arisen very recently and has changed the focus of the use of teaching assistants.

As previously stated, the teaching assistant is employed to undertake a variety of tasks. www.motionsworld (2003) indicates that they:

> undertake a wide range of tasks, many within the classroom, but also elsewhere in the school. Out of class tasks may include those with an emphasis on care, such as first aid, playground supervision and those with a more administrative emphasis such as taking responsibility for the library or other resource areas.

More crucially, Lorenz (1998) provides us with the figures that for 28 per cent of primary aged children with Down's syndrome, 'almost all direct teaching is carried out by support assistants'. This is an area of support that requires a more explicit infrastructure in order to maximize expertise in teaching and support roles.

It is tempting, when struggling with the demands of a large class, to ask the teaching assistant to undertake tasks such as hearing struggling readers or just to sit with a group to help them with their work. If this is to be a meaningful activity for the children it takes skill to listen to children, pick up on their miscues and to determine how to intervene or best support the child. Teaching assistants may tell children to 'sound it out' when attempting to read a word which could not be sounded out or, conversely, just tell the child every word they stumble on, thus not developing any independent reading strategies at all. In such classrooms there is likely to be dissatisfaction with the job and the teaching assistant may feel undervalued, as reported by a government-commissioned report (cited by Nursery World, 2001 – http://www.literacytrust.org.uk/database/teachassist.html).

It may help to ask certain questions when working with a teaching assistant:

● What do I want the outcome of working with a teaching assistant to be in the next term?

● Do I want extra time/support for particular groups of children?

● Do I want the chance to spend time undertaking, for example, focused observations or in-depth conferences?

● Do I want the teaching assistant to clear the backlog of paperwork, and can he or she do this without my being there?

● Do I want to improve the environment and make the room tidier/the displays more dynamic, etc. – all the things I don't currently have time to do to a high level?

● Do I want to leave a list of things to do or do I want to liaise with this person about teaching and learning?

● What are my deficiencies and can the teaching assistant complete these in any way?

To get the best out of the teaching assistant, the teacher needs to be clear about why he or she wants a teaching assistant and the skills and aptitudes of the teaching assistant need to be recognized. DfES (2000) also indicates that the role may 'require more thought than it does for any other member of staff whose role is better established. It may also require more monitoring and follow up'.

●●● Skills and personal qualities required for working with children with SEN

In order to work with small groups of children supporting learning, teaching assistants need the ability to:

● think laterally – to reinterpret material if not understood the first time;

● reinterpret without becoming frustrated;

● work within a timescale, keeping the children focused;

● recognize when a child is ready to move on;

● manage children and bring them back on task;

● work completely independently for a short time.

They also need the following:

- Patience and an understanding that children do not necessarily learn from the first experience.
- An understanding of the impact that having difficulty learning has on other aspects of life.
- The capacity to learn from the teacher and from the learner.
- The capacity to observe children and to report back.
- The capacity to evaluate when and how a child has learnt or not learnt a concept and where the point of difficulty lies.
- Knowledge of certain aspects of learning development and, if working with particular groups, the main features of their learning disability (Hall 2004).

Personal qualities of a teaching assistant working with children who have special needs are important, too.

He or she needs to be:

- approachable while maintaining a dignified distance so that he or she is able to empathize with children, be more child focused while being able to manage the curriculum from the adult perspective;
- discreet about information received.

Teaching assistants need professionalism in working as part of a team even if they do not 'get on' with the teacher on a personal or social level.

They need to know:

- when to pass on certain information;
- the right level of intimacy with children, as many teaching assistants are known to children outside school;
- how to be reflective and how to work with the teacher in evaluating all aspects of delivering a task; and
- how important and central they are to the activity of learning.

Fox (1998) identifies the essential qualities and knowledge a teaching assistant must possess as 'Patience, care, sense of fairness, consistency, flexibility, positive attitudes, versatility, ability to learn from mistakes, friendliness, being hard to shock, sense of humour and enthusiasm'.

Finally, the DfES (2000) suggests that parents should be informed of school policy on employing teaching assistants who support special needs children. They should know who the individual teaching assistants are and their responsibilities. This DfES policy document provides valuable information for clarifying the job descriptions and good practice of teaching assistants.

●●● The 'non-teaching' teaching assistant

A 'non-teaching' teaching assistant who supports children with special needs may undertake work which is necessary and integral to the task of teaching but may not involve direct contact with the children. This may include mounting pupils' work, helping to prepare specific materials for children with special needs (such as enlarged or adapted texts) or it may involve contact with children on a personal support level, helping them to change for PE or helping with personal hygiene matters, for example. The skills and qualities of a non-teaching teaching assistant may be completely different from those needed by a teaching assistant who does teach.

The non-teaching teaching assistant who is used to reduce the workload of routine jobs needs to be:

- able to work independently for short spells of time;
- creative in carrying out tasks, such as displays;
- able to manage his or her own time with a set amount of work to be completed within a given timescale;
- self-motivated as there is little feedback from wall displays or neatly filed records;
- able to work as an 'invisible' member of the environment as sometimes he or she will be working in a class while a lesson is being taken but he or she is not part of that lesson; and
- able to follow instructions accurately.

The personal qualities may also be different for this person. For example, he or she will need to be:

- discreet about information overheard;
- flexible and adaptable, being able to work for a variety of different teachers;
- honest about his or her skills, know what he or she can and cannot do;

- able to look at the work of others to pick up and adapt ideas;
- able to work with a certain amount of initiative and;
- more adult focused than child focused but still be able to see the classroom from a child's perspective.

Woodward and Smithers (*Guardian* 17 September 2002) report that David Bell, the head of Ofsted, indicated his belief that the boundaries between teachers and assistants should be preserved. There is also the potential for different levels of teaching assistants, some of whom have taken further training to work with children directly, while others (who are happy with a more peripheral role) work alongside the teacher but not directly in a teaching capacity (this aspect is discussed later).

●●● Relationships

Hopefully, teachers will develop a warm and trusting relationship with teaching assistants based on mutual respect and recognition of each other's strengths and weaknesses. However, this will not happen automatically in all classrooms and, in some instances, some hard work has to be invested to make the relationship work. One of the most difficult scenarios is the newly qualified teacher who must work with an older and more experienced teaching assistant (see Chapter 7).

Working with another adult in the room is a very personal experience and it requires ease between the two people. If differences and resentments are allowed to grow, then neither teacher nor teaching assistant can function to his or her best and the children may suffer. Ideally, a daily review would provide feedback and forward planning when a new teaching assistant is first brought into the class or when a new teacher takes up post in a class with a resident teaching assistant. In the case of newly appointed teachers within a stable setting, once the teacher has settled with the class it may be a good idea to search out an approachable person and ask for advice in dealing with the teaching assistant and ask how other teachers manage their teaching assistants. Often one teaching assistant may work across several classes, and other teachers may have strategies for peaceful living that are worth noting. What of the relationship between pupil and teaching assistant?

●●● Pupil relationships with classroom assistants

Teaching assistants often have a special relationship with the pupils they encounter if they have a supported teaching role, especially when this is with children with special educational needs. These relationships are crucially important. A child who is unhappy will not learn. Arguably, adults can bring about a great deal of children's happy disposition at school. The teacher or teaching assistant has the power to make learning interesting, fun and worth while or to make it tedious, mundane and uninteresting, and a meaningless chore. Many excellent teaching assistants have realized that, for children, the primary aim of life is to have fun. They make light of situations when it would have been possible to use a heavy hand, and they manage children with humour and understanding – recognizing that you cannot force a child to do anything and, once you have reached the stage of using force, you have lost credibility. Getting children to do what is required is about developing a relationship so that the child does want to please and respect adults in the classroom. The good manager of children will laugh with the children, celebrate their successes and show children how well they have done when they do not realize it themselves. They will also not be afraid to set limits, to let the children know those limits, to react if the children overstep the boundaries of those limits. The reward for complying is being with that person and the sanction is to be out of favour with that person. When a teaching assistant works continuously with the same group of children with special needs, this relationship becomes even more important. It can prompt children to look forward to working or can engender strategies of avoidance.

The teaching assistant can often develop a close relationship with the children he or she is working with and can become a valuable channel for information that would be less well received from a teacher. He or she may be very valuable in addressing sensitive issues in drugs education, sexuality and child protection issues. Equally, he or she can provide the teacher with insights about the children.

●●● Strengths and weaknesses of working as a team

Working with another adult is not new for many people these days. The era of the closed classroom door with a single teacher in the room is fast disappearing. In the early years, most teachers are used to working with support in the classroom for part of the time. This is a relatively new situation for Key Stage 2 and secondary teachers. However, even here there has been a steadily growing stream of extra individuals who work alongside the teacher.

Working with another adult in the room, especially when supporting the most vulnerable pupils, requires skill and sensitivity. The teacher may be under scrutiny regarding his or her teaching and discipline. For some people, this may feel like being on permanent school experience! It may be humiliating for teaching assistants when they have difficulty with a group of children or when he or she is trying to encourage a particular child to finish work and is being observed by the teacher. The nuts and bolts of working with another person in the room come to the fore when extraordinary happenings occur, for example behaviour is handled badly. The other adult in the classroom can be used to defuse a situation or as a resource to take the heat out of an incident, as long as this has been agreed beforehand as a suitable role. It would obviously not be appropriate for a teacher to send a badly behaved child to a new teaching assistant but, when a teacher recognizes that a teaching assistant may have a particular 'way' with a child, it may be profitable to assign that teaching assistant to modifying the behaviour. Indeed, many teaching assistants are assigned to children with challenging behaviour for this very purpose. A post-mortem discussion afterwards is often helpful: each can admit vulnerabilities and ponder on how others have managed particularly difficult children. A more difficult position to manage is when a teaching assistant fails to manage disruptive behaviour that impacts on the groups being taught by the teacher. In this situation it is necessary for the teacher to find an approach which will remove the troublesome child from the group while at the same time, maintaining the dignity and standing of the teaching assistant. If the teacher cannot manage the troublesome child any better than the teaching assistant, the child should be left in the group and the teacher should find focusing strategies for the remainder of the class and deal with the pupil alone later, in isolation from the rest of the class. It is imperative that the teacher does not humiliate the teaching assistant or allow him or her to be seen as incapable by the pupils, as this could have repercussions later. The responsibility and skills needed of the teacher working with a variety of teaching assistants are extensive. They need to be able to manage other adults, to prioritize and rationalize work, to make explicit their wishes and intentions and, at the same time, to monitor the effectiveness of the adults working under their supervision. In effect there is a second layer of skills; those of the manager have been added to the role of educator of children. I will now address some of these issues.

●●● Delegating classroom tasks

A slightly different aspect of working as a team is the management of another's workload. This is not something most teachers feel comfortable with or are prepared for in training. However, this is a very real situation in most classes. Some teachers are arguably not very good at asking for help or at delegating tasks, as this is often seen as a sign of weakness. The new consultant image Estelle Morris visualized needs just those abilities. Setting the tasks for the teaching assistant should not be a task undertaken by the teacher without reference to the teaching assistant. There are four main types of task in a classroom that need to be delegated:

1 Teaching small groups
2 Social needs, such as cleaning up or changing children.
3 Undertaking 'important administrative tasks', such as keeping a check of exam and test results and entering marks on computers.
4 Essential but menial tasks, such as washing the paint pots.

Reserving the most sensitive and informed teaching assistant to use with pupils with special needs may also be a good strategy.

If you have a 'to do' board everyone who is part of your team can see, whenever there is a lull no one's time is wasted. Often teaching assistants sit at the side of the room when they do not need to be there – they are only there waiting for the word 'go'. There are always jobs to be done either by the teacher or the teaching assistant, and a priority group of children who need more attention and support.

Sometimes it is more beneficial for the teaching assistant to remove a small group of children to undertake extra work than for these children to sit in the same room as the rest of the class, gradually becoming more and more bored with the lesson content, which seems to have little relevance to them. This, however, needs careful forethought and planning.

●●● Curriculum planning

When using a teaching assistant who supports children with special needs, it will be necessary for the teacher to share his or her thoughts about how to teach the group if the teaching assistant is to have a valuable input into planning for the group. It is good practice to discuss planning and to share ideas about what happens if a child gets 'stuck' and to suggest alternative ways of explaining a problem and extension activities if the children finish early: 'The teacher and teaching assistant combine to make a team by clear communication and regular discussions' ('Advice for teachers working with a teaching assistant' – www. specialschool.org). An explanation of the outcomes, including any vocabulary required by the session, not just the content, is required. The DfES (2000) informs us that 'all the evidence shows that the team of teacher and TA works at its highest level when the TA is informed by the teacher of the plans and intentions for the lesson and is consulted over their execution'. However, this aspect was one of the concerns raised as part of the evaluation of the SCRE pilot project: that finding time remained problematic even in schools where there was management support for the initiative (Wilson *et al.*, 2003).

Teachers also need to give the teaching assistant information about the children with special needs, detailing their preferred way of working and specific difficulties relating to their special need. Many assistants who work with children who have special needs do not know the exact details of the child's needs, only that he or she has 'special needs'. This is often due to confidentiality issues. If teaching assistants are to be considered part of a professional team they need access to essential information. One would not expect to turn up at the doctor's surgery to be treated by a nurse who does not have all the facts. There are, however, ethical issues involved, and teaching assistants need to be prepared and trained in these issues.

This curriculum planning takes time, and time should be taken afterwards to gain the teaching assistant's opinion about how well the group did. Similarly, many of the training days for literacy and numeracy support target teachers but not teaching assistants. In many cases it will be teaching assistants who undertake the work with pupils with special needs, and it would be good practice and sensible to include teaching assistants in further training.

●●● Training and professional development

The DfEE (1997) noted that the greater reliance being placed on the use of teaching assistants now 'makes training and career development essential'. However, the same source details that Ofsted found that fewer than a half of all LEAs provided relevant training for teaching assistants even though there are now widely available training courses at various levels, including specialist courses for teaching assistants who support dyslexic pupils. Those who are supported by accreditation through the West of England Psychology Services (http://weps.co.uk/classroom-assistants.html) and National Vocational Qualifications (NVQs) (www.lg-employers.gov.uk/skills/teaching), have courses specifically tailored for teaching assistants in the use of ICT (www.pearsoninformation.co.uk/courses/ClassAssistants.html) all of which have been approved for funding through the Standards Fund (£350 million was available between 1999 and 2002). Recently the first national awards for classroom assistants came about. It is to be hoped that all these valuable members of the school community will soon be given not only the recognition they deserve but also the training to make them more effective.

All in-service workshops and sessions that seem relevant to the role of the teaching assistants should be available to them, or they should receive regular in-school feedback from the teachers who have attended them. A word of caution is needed here, however. If some teaching assistants attend courses and others do not, it is possible that a double layer of teaching assistants is created, with a certain amount of prestige going to those who have attended. In these circumstances an agreed rationale about roles from the outset, in consultation with the relevant teaching assistants, will have its advantages. Many teaching assistants take this route into teaching, having missed out on the usual route early in their careers. Many teaching assistants are happy to sustain a less developed role within schools but can still fulfil valuable roles, while others actively seek to be more informed and better qualified. There has to be room for both.

●●● Practical ideas for working with teaching assistants

When working in the classroom with classroom assistants, there are always unforeseen situations. I have found the following strategies and devices useful here:

- At the start of each week, identify certain children who need to be high profile, those who require support in reading and children who need extra consolidation or in-depth observation.
- These names could go on the wall, with a daily tick sheet to indicate whether extra help has been given.
- Classroom assistants could consult the list and identify the next child available for extra help.
- Make available a 'fall back' box of activities or system of extra activities for the teaching assistant to use at a moment's notice.

- Make available a 'what should I do now?' box. This could contain adult assisted activities, such as simple reinforcement tasks.

- Play/construction activity cards can be linked to aspects of the curriculum, such as buildings that require the child to identify solids, name shapes or count blocks.

- For some children, individual folders to be used and followed so that the next few aspects of the learning that are to be consolidated are ready in the file for the teaching assistant to access. These could include fun activities and brain teasers, as well as more mundane worksheets.

- Make available teacher-designed games that could be used at a variety of levels depending on the ability of the children and the level of support available.

- Make a note of a piece of work that needs further explanation at some point.

This system could be applied to any extra tuition needed, be it reading or maths, as long as the list of children and the activities are relatively public and the materials readily available. Individual education plans could be accessible along with teaching plans, if appropriate.

●●● Summary and conclusion

Given that the government is committed to recruiting 50,000 extra teaching and teaching assistants by 2006 (Smithers, *Guardian* 18 October 2002), arguably the best use of teaching assistants can be achieved when they are properly briefed about the learning outcomes, content and appropriate styles of presentation for the group of pupils with whom they will be working. The frequent use of teaching assistants in supporting children who have special needs requires high levels of personal skills and the ability to empathize with the various difficulties encountered by children. It is untenable for the most needy pupils to be entrusted to the least qualified person in the room. It is the duty of the teacher to ensure that the teaching assistants can undertake the task of supporting children with special needs at least as well as he or she can, otherwise there is no rationale for having a teaching assistant working with these children (for further details of special educational needs and the role of the teaching assistant, see Hall, 2004). A well informed teaching assistant and a teacher willing to make the most of the partnership will ultimately raise the standard of all pupils, not just the most capable. They can make inclusion a reality in every classroom, not just a word to be emblazoned on documents.

●●● References

BBC Education (2001)(http://news.bbc.co.uk/1/hi/eduteaching assistanttion/165.1653.stm).

Curtis, P. (2002) 'Assistants not benefiting teachers,' *Guardian*, 16 April.

DfEE (1997) *Learning Support Assistants* (green paper) (http://www.inclusive.co.uk/greenpap/lsas.shtml).

DfES (2000) *Working with Teaching Assistants*. London: HMSO.

Fox, G. (1998) *A Handbook for Learning Support Assistants: Teachers and Assistants Working Together*. London: David Fulton.

Hall, W. (2004) 'Inclusion – special needs', in C. Bold (ed.) *Supporting Teaching and Learning*. London: David Fulton.

Kerry, T. (2002) 'The road to hell…but no way back' (http://www.sourceuk.net/articles/a02083.html).

Lorenz, S. (1998) *Children with Down's Syndrome: A Guide for Teachers and Support Assistants in Mainstream Education*. London: David Fulton.

Mercer, A. (2002) 'Teachers express views on assistants' (www.nursery-world.co.uk/news/main.asp?ID=2198).

Motionsworld (2003) 'What is a classroom assistant?' (http://www.motionsworld.pwp.blueyonder.co.uk/classroomassistant/role_of_teaching assistant.htm).

NASEN (2002) 'Policy on learning support assistants' (http://www.nasen.org.uk/policy/15/pg02.htm)

SCRE (2001) *Classroom Assistant Evaluation Report – 'A Little Bit of Sunshine' – Classroom Assistant Evaluation Report*. (http://egfl.net/Teaching/Issues/CLASSROOM ASSISTANTevaluation/ACReport.htm)

Wilson, V., Schlapp, U. and Davidson, J. (2003) 'Insight 1: classroom assistants: key issues from the national evaluation' (http://www.scotland.gov.uk/library5/eduteaching assistanttion/Insi-00.asp).

●●● Chapter 4

Learning mentors in primary classrooms and schools

Pat Hughes

Ten years ago it would have been rare to find learning mentors in the English education system. In this chapter I look at their introduction and growth in primary schools, examine the training given and explore their role in one school. I hope to show how this particular initiative has produced a very distinctive 'new' professional in primary schools.

●●● Background

Learning mentors form one strand of the Department for Education and Skills (DfES) Excellence in Cities programme. This expanding initiative was introduced in March 1999 to tackle 'specific problems' facing children in our cities. Through a combination of initiatives, the Excellence in Cities programme aimed to raise the aspirations and achievements of pupils and to tackle disaffection, social exclusion, truancy and indiscipline and to improve parents' confidence in cities.

Initially the six key strands of the Excellence in Cities programme focused on secondary schools in six conurbations – inner London, Birmingham, Manchester and Salford, Liverpool and Knowsley, Leeds and Bradford and Sheffield and Rotherham. The six strands covered the following:

1 Learning mentors for all pupils who needed them.
2 The creation of learning support units.
3 The development of city learning centres.

4 The creation of more beacon and specialist schools.

5 The expansion of small Excellence in Cities action zones.

6 Extended opportunities for gifted and talented pupils.

The strands were based on what the DfES described as 'core values'. These were high expectations, diversity, networks and extension of opportunity. The subtext might also be that, despite attempts by both the Conservative and Labour governments to tackle the educational and social problems of the major cities in England, these areas remained largely untouched by central government initiatives. Political statements made about the need to raise achievement in economically deprived areas continued to remain as statements rather than be translated into a focused programme. Ofsted continued to find a much greater proportion of schools in these areas as being in need of special measures. Levels of attainment as monitored via GCSE and Key Stage 2 SATs results were lower. A political agenda of 'Education, education and education' had to deliver more than platitudes. All political parties, in particular the Labour Party, have a long tradition of seeing education as 'a way out' of the poverty cycle. This particular education initiative can be seen very much in terms of this 'Old Labour' belief in the power of education to change lives.

The Excellence in Cities initiative used good practice from projects from within the UK, but also imported ideas from the USA (e.g. magnet schools). The programme was largely met with enthusiasm by the schools in these areas, who saw it as a recognition that more than words were needed to raise aspirations and hope for pupils in their schools.

The second phase of the learning mentor programme (September 2000) expanded geographically to 22 new LEAs. It was also extended on a pilot basis into some primary schools within the original six partnerships. At the time of writing, the programme is continuing to expand into other areas in the country in both the primary and secondary sectors. A National Training Programme for mentors was established in 2001 and materials for this programme have been updated and revised each year (Liverpool Excellence Partnership, 2003). The programme provides mentors with a formal qualification.

The rapid expansion of the learning mentor programme can be seen as a mark of its success, but it is only a long-term evaluation that can really monitor the effectiveness on individual pupils' life chances. Fortunately the partnerships themselves have a vested interest in monitoring value for money and Excellence in Cities action plans are required to evaluate initiatives on an ongoing basis.

They are also expected to identify the total level of expenditure on learning mentors; specify and prioritize the types of barriers to learning; reach agreement among the cluster schools about distribution of funding; provide plans for monitoring progress; provide networking facilities for mentors; and ensure that learning mentors complement but do not duplicate other services. The Excellence in Cities cluster plans had to make certain provision that the learning mentors added value to related initiatives and could demonstrate that.

The primary Excellence in Cities policy covered three specific strands:

1 Learning mentors.
2 Primary learning support units (PLSU's).
3 Gifted and talented children.

Primary headteachers in the Excellence in Cities areas involved were seconded to manage the programme and ensure that the essential primary, local expertise was available in the recruitment, training and management of the learning mentors. The Excellence in Cities partnerships tackled this in different ways. Birmingham LEA, for example, identified five key objectives for its primary learning mentor programme:

1 Ensuring that all pupils who need one will have access to a 'professionally trained' learning mentor to remove barriers to learning, both within and outside school.
2 Targeting help on those who need it most, particularly pupils who are experiencing multiple disadvantages.
3 Raising standards and reducing truancy and exclusion.
4 Building up networks which include existing community-based voluntary mentor schemes as well as extending employment opportunities for local people.
5 Providing a complementary service to existing school staff, and to others providing services outside school, to help pupils to access the help that they need (http://www.bgfl.org/services/mentors/default/html).

The Liverpool website on learning mentors (www.liverpoolmentors.org.uk) recognized that each learning mentor will work in a different way to address priorities set out by the school. The website gives some examples of the kinds of areas in which the learning mentors are already working within primary schools:

- Improving attendance and punctuality.
- Primary support centres.
- Modifying children's behaviour.
- Helping children to understand health-related issues, such as going to bed early.
- Encouraging children to play more appropriately.
- Helping children to cope with conflict.
- Supporting the class teacher in identifying reasons for slow learning progress.

In October 2002, an evaluation report on the primary learning mentor strand of Excellence in Cities (Hobson and Kington, 2002) identified major benefits of the scheme, although their findings did acknowledge considerable differences between the work of mentors in different schools, different types of partnerships and the concern of some headteachers about the continued funding. But the overall evaluation has identified that this particular strand of the Excellence in Cities initiative has been an overwhelming success and many headteachers were using school funding to pay for additional mentoring support.

●●● The role of the learning mentor

The DfES has published general guidelines for the role of learning mentors and, as we have seen from the Liverpool and Birmingham websites, there is likely to be a local tone to job specifications as well as a school one. The differences here are very much in the wording and priorities rather than the philosophy of the role of the learning mentor.

The learning mentor is seen as being a key person in helping individual pupils to overcome barriers to learning and acting as an advocate for pupils. These barriers are recognized as being both within and outside school. The mentor role is to support pupils 'who are at risk of underachieving or disengaging from learning for a variety of reasons'. Learning mentors are seen as key personnel to assess why pupils are experiencing barriers to learning and the guidelines recognize that these can include a range of factors, such as feeling demotivated, lacking in self-esteem and falling behind with their work.

The guidance (www.standards.dfes.gov.uk/exellence/policies/mentors) suggests that learning mentors will:

- Target help on those who need it most, especially those suffering multiple disadvantage;
- Raise standards and reduce truancy and exclusion – helping schools make accelerated progress towards achieving local attainment, truancy, exclusion and other relevant targets;
- Provide a complementary service to existing school staff, and to other providing services outside school, to help pupils to access the help that they need.

Learning mentor functions are wide-ranging and the skills needed are complex. Many functions at one time would have been seen as part of the teacher's role. For example, the DfES guidelines for learning mentor functions identify the transfer of information and assessment. This at one time would have been firmly in the hands of the Y2 and Y6 teacher. The DfES now sees that this can be part of the role of the learning mentor. Other potential functions can include the following

- One-to-one mentoring and support, which can involve drawing up and implementing an action plan for each child, unless the child already has such a plan.
- Working with families of children receiving this support to encourage positive family involvement.
- Building up a database of the range of support available for pupils – out-of-school study, social services, for example.
- Working with voluntary mentors. Often in the primary sector, this can include community groups coming in to work with children with reading difficulties.

Individual school specifications will reflect the specific needs of that school and are likely to be adapted and changed as the role of the learning mentor becomes more institutionalized. Certainly, as a primary governor on the appointments panel for two learning mentors in the first phase, I had very little idea of how their role would translate into reality. I also had concerns about the relatively high rate of pay, which matched that of a newly qualified teacher, and also the need for specialist training. The initial salaries paid meant that recruitment could take place from a wide range of backgrounds. This included teachers (but excluded teachers in the same school as the mentoring post), teaching assistants, nursery nurses, education welfare officers and social workers. Confidentiality, child protection, induction, training and monitoring continue to be seen as key markers in identifying the success of the initiative as a whole as well as the success of individual mentors.

●●● Induction and training

The first learning mentors appointed into primary school came from a variety of backgrounds (Hobson and Kington, 2002), and this pattern has continued. Initial induction and training took place in schools and within the Excellence in Cities clusters. By January 2001, there was a national five-day training programme in place. This had been designed to ensure that all primary learning mentors had the skills needed to carry out their duties. It was developed by the Liverpool Excellence Partnership, published by the DfEE, and provided excellent information and support for anyone working in an educational setting. It covered four modules:

1 The primary school as a learning organization – its structure, literacy and numeracy strategies, the management of inclusion.
2 The role of the learning mentor – enhancing personal and professional effectiveness; child protection; statutory frameworks for health and safety and workplace regulations; the 'extended' role of the learning mentor; managing transition; and the role of external providers.
3 The nature of children's learning – learning hand in hand with development; working with diversity in learning; educational support services; enhancing children's motivation; and monitoring and assessing children's learning.
4 Supporting children and their families – basic helping skills; working with children on their behaviour; addressing emotional growth; fostering personal, social and emotional development through circle time; and developing home–school liaison.

All mentors were expected to take part in this training course, which was delivered locally. The training was updated in September 2003, when the pattern of learning mentors had become more established and other priorities for primary learning mentors had come into focus. These included the underachieving gifted and talented pupils and strategies to support boys' learning.

●●● Matthew's story

Background

Matthew (a fictional name) was one of the very first primary mentors appointed when the pilot initiative started in primary schools. He was appointed as one of two full-time mentors to a school which had just been identified by Ofsted as having serious weaknesses. The school had – and still does have – over 75 per cent of its pupil role of 350 children in receipt of free school dinners and is in an LEA with one of the most deprived populations in Europe. The mentor appointed with him left after 18 months, and the person appointed in her place only stayed in post for a week. Since then he has worked as the sole mentor in the school.

The following is an account of Matthew's experience, told in his own words.

Prior experience

Before my appointment, I was driving a cab and had just finished a business degree with the Open University. This had started as a Higher National Diploma in business finance at the local college. After doing the degree, I had originally thought about going into marketing, but then decided to go for a Post-graduate Certificate in Education. I then spent some time working voluntarily in the classroom with a teacher whom I knew well because he had been at the school when I was a pupil here. I spent time in the classroom and working outside with the children. When the learning mentor's post came up, the class teacher suggested that I apply for it. There were 35 mentors appointed in the LEA then and we all had degrees. Quite a few have now left. There are now mentors in nearly every school in the authority. My appointment is to this school and the headteacher is my manager. Initially, another member of the senior management team acted as the mentor co-ordinator. This was part of his general mentoring role with student teachers and newly qualified teachers.

Job specification

Initially, there was no job specification and the post was very vague. Basically it was to 'break down barriers to learning'. After a couple of months, the head drew up a job specification, which we all agreed on and this is still the same one as I have now. A primary headteacher from another school in the LEA was seconded part time to run the mentor programme and advised us to get into school and get to know how primary schools worked. It was made clear that we were professionals and that we needed to ensure that teachers saw us as professionals, and not just as a new type of classroom assistant.

Getting the teachers on board took a long time, at least 18 months. This was for a number of reasons. The initiative was a new one and no one had any experience of what a primary mentor was expected to do. Primary teachers have a very personal relationship with their classes and were not sure how the presence of a mentor would change this. Teachers were anxious that we would take away precious teaching time and this would influence school attainment in the Standard Assessment Tasks. Teachers were telling children what to do and expected all children to follow their instructions. As mentors, we were rewarding some pupils for doing what was expected of all children. For example, with attendance we were giving certificates in a weekly assembly to children whose attendance had moved from 70 per cent to 80 per cent, but not rewarding any of the others whose attendance had improved as well. Now we still give certificates to these very poor attenders when their attendance is better, but do not do it in assembly. This makes it less obvious.

Initially teachers did not like us taking children out of the classroom to work with. It has taken time to build up the relationship, so that teachers are now referring children to me, are happy for me to work in the classroom with individuals, groups and sometimes with the whole class. They are also happy to let some children come out of the classroom. Now the relationships are fine. I have more access to children and teachers are very proactive about referring children to me, particularly about attendance. I have given presentations to the governors who were also not sure what a learning mentor did. This recognition of my post has taken about a year to 18 months.

Training

All the first mentors were 'put in cold' into school. We were advised to get to know the school and then had some specific mentor training. Since then, we have had a lot more training. This has included focused mentor training with the local authority and shared training with the teacher. The headteacher has let me go on courses which have been identified as being useful, either by staff or me. These have included sessions on awareness about drugs use, child protection, counselling, circle time, first aid, citizenship, football and cricket coaching and helping children to cope with grief. These courses have mostly been in the evenings and half-term. The network meetings of mentors have enabled us to identify specific training needs, such as handling and restraint.

Establishing a database

One of the original primary learning mentors has now become a link co-ordinator for the learning mentor scheme and is based with the other advisory and curriculum support teams. She attends the half-termly mentor clusters, which are very important. They enable us to network, share information and identify issues common to us all. At the moment we are working on trying to ensure that our referral and procedural documentation is all the same. This has had difficulties, because some mentors are in schools, where the documentation is already fixed and the heads do not want to change it.

Figure 4.1 is a template of the current database.

Attendance

Attendance and punctuality are big problems in this school and remain a key priority. About a quarter of the school have an attendance record of 90 per cent or less. This creates a roll of 150–160 children. It is worse in the Nursery and Reception, which we include because we think good attendance is a habit learnt from an early age. We have some large families with several children in the school, who may all be absent at the same time.

Teachers find it difficult to teach children who have poor attendance and also those who arrive late. Basically we set up and run the procedures to improve this. There were already some in place, for example the weekly attendance shield for the class with the best attendance. Children now get a 100 per cent attendance certificate if every child in the class is there all week. This uses peer pressure to encourage children to come to school. As well as the attendance certificates we established early-bird cards to encourage punctuality. I am timetabled every morning after the registers have been taken to contact families where children are absent and whose general attendance record is a cause for concern. If it does not improve the education welfare officer is informed. I have a good relationship with the education welfare officer, who is very generous with his time. If there is still no improvement, parents and carers receive a caution letter. This gradual build-up generally succeeds with the majority of the pupils, but does leave us with a hard core of about 36 children whose attendance is 85 per cent or below. This is a very real problem as, until the recent court cases, which resulted in parents being imprisoned, most parents recognized that the threat to go to court and even court appearances were an empty threat.

The 85 per cent attendance record is seen as our cut-off point, although obviously we are working less formally with all those whose attendance is poor. Teachers very often refer children, whose general attendance is better than 85 per cent, but who are missing too much school. Sometimes brothers and sisters have different attendance rates.

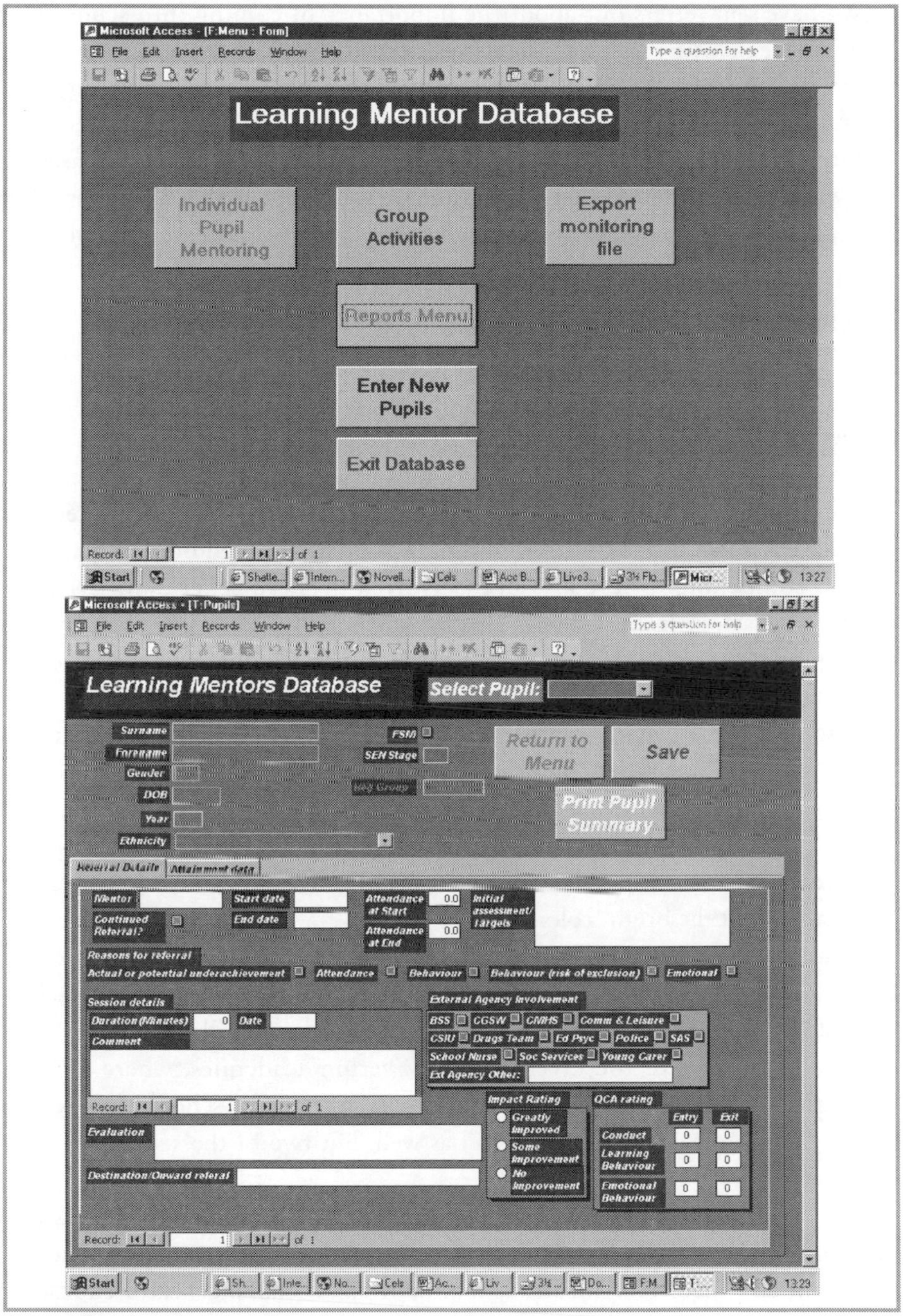

■ **Figure 4.1**
A template of the current database

We have sent letters out about the importance of coming into school first thing in the morning, so that parents realize that their children miss important things if they are not there. For the past two years, we have piloted a very successful breakfast club during SATs weeks and often had 100 per cent of the children attending. We did try to establish this on a more permanent basis the following term, but found that after a time we were only getting a very few children and it was just not an effective use of time. Some schools are still doing it.

Behaviour

It is about getting children to take responsibility for their own actions. As soon as they accept that responsibility and realize that it is their own actions which are causing problems, the easier it becomes to solve behavioural difficulties. This has involved a great deal of counselling work, which I am very interested in. I have had additional training and have started on an additional qualification in counselling. I have also been involved in more generic initiatives to improve behaviour in the school. This has included work on positive play and development of the playground from a black tarmac area into somewhere exciting for the children to play. The Key Stage 2 playground has now got football pens so that those playing football do not take over the whole playground as the balls do not hurt other children. This gives more room for other play activities and quiet areas with benches. On the infant playground we have just had painted games and visual learning support such as a map of the UK. This has been really successful, apart from someone who lives opposite coming in to complain about the bright colours!

I am in the playground at the start of the day and at playtime and lunchtime. I am also involved with positive play initiatives after school, such as football, cross-country runs and last term we had circus skills. We make good use of the facilities of the Liverpool and Everton academies, where football competitions are organized. The school is also in the local schools' leagues for sports. I used to run the girls' football as well, but two of the staff have taken this over.

I have been involved with training welfare staff in encouraging positive playgroup behaviour and both they and I have modelled positive play activities. I am also involved with the school personal, social and health education programme (PSHE) and the citizenship initiative. The mentor budget has been used to buy additional resources and I work closely with the PSHE co-ordinator. This is going very well and has covered areas such as drugs, drinking, smoking and safety in the home. Most classes have circle time and I have modelled good practice for others and given ideas for circle time, as well as being able to suggest resources and provide a good foundation text for teachers to use. The school now has a Schools Council and is part of the LEA Children's Parliament.

Parents

I am in the playground every morning before school and after school, and parents will often come and see me then. Sometimes this is to pass a message on to the teachers, and this frees the teachers to welcome children into the classroom at the start of the day. Not long after our initial appointment, in order to make it clear what our roles were, we produced a short leaflet about 'learning mentors' at the school for pupils and parents. This covered questions they were asking, such as:

- What is a mentor?
- What is a learning mentor?
- What happens when a child goes to see a learning mentor?
- What does a learning mentor do?
- Can a learning mentor help parents?

Obviously learning mentors need to have regular contact with parents and carers and it is part of our role to give support to families who would benefit from the involvement of a mentor. I also work with parents in relation to transition to secondary school and to special schools and have helped them with appeals when they disagree with the decision about their child. I have helped parents compile curriculum vitae when they are looking for work, and discussed strategies to improve children's behaviour, both at school and at home. I also provide them with information about courses in the local area, which they might like to attend.

I know many of the parents because I was at school with them and, like them, still live in the area. This has advantages and disadvantages. I was once asked to give support to a father whose son was in trouble for bullying. He wanted me to say that his child was not a bully and he thought I would do this because he knew me at school. I could not do that. The situation was difficult and I was physically threatened. Fortunately this is rare and the child in this case has transferred to another school. I also work with the Friends of the School and they have given funds for different things such as football kits.

Outside agencies

I work with several outside agencies. These include case conferences for special educational needs reviews, the Pupil Referral Centre, and secondary and special schools where transition is involved. I also distribute materials produced by the local authority. For example, the council produced a leaflet for parents and children about road safety skills and, like the transition leaflet, I worked through this with the children.

Budget

Initially we had a start-up budget from the LEA. This was generous and enabled us to get the office equipment and furniture we needed, as well as create a good environment where children could come and see us. We have bought a lot of resources, both for the mentor programmes with individual and groups of children, and for classrooms. These have included wet playtime kits, resources for new initiatives such as PSHE, citizenship, circle time and healthy schools. Over time, the budget has gone down, but the headteacher here is very supportive and will give some additional money.

●●● Commentary

Matthew has now been in post three years. He has established himself well in the school. Teachers, governors and other adults working there understand his role in relation to themselves and the pupils. He provides a useful male role model in an area where many pupils do not have a fixed male model in their lives. This is particularly important in primary schools were there are few, if any, male teachers or support workers. It moves primary schooling out of its 'women's world' ethos (Hodgeon, 1991) and gives both boys and girls an opportunity to relate to an adult male.

His connections with the local community are important as he is seen as part of that the community. Many of the other adult support workers live in the community, but none of the teachers do. His personal experience of education has given him an opportunity to gain a degree and some element of choice about what he does. This is reflected in his interest in helping parents to gain access to qualifications which will make them more employable. He also has 'street cred', which the 22-year-old newly qualified teacher, travelling in and out of the area, may take several years to establish.

Attendance and punctuality at the school have improved, but this is an ongoing problem faced by many schools in Excellence in Cities clusters. His role as a counsellor is likely to extend as yet more evidence comes to light about the mental health of primary school children. He sees his future career in this light.

The mentor as counsellor is very much in line with American elementary school practice. Many schools in the USA have counsellors in post, either full time or shared with a number of other schools. This acknowledges that many of the 'barriers to learning' are linked to individual children's needs. Teachers, however inspirational and motivating, have difficulty in reaching children whose social and emotional needs are not being met, either at home or at school.

The growth in the role of the mentor is a good reminder that we all need to acknowledge that Maslow's theory of basic needs (1962) has continuing relevance in our schools today. The role of the mentor as advocate and counsellor is designed to make that difference to individuals. Let us hope that government cuts in funding to schools do not effect the development of their role.

●●● References

DfES (2001) *Guidance for Learning Mentors*. London: DfES.

Hobson, A. and Kington, A. (2002) *Evaluation of Excellence in Cities Primary Extension: A Report on the Findings of the Learning Mentor Strand Study* (www.nfer.ac.uk/research/eic.asp).

Hodgeon, J. (1985) *A Woman's World*. Cleveland LEA.

Liverpool Excellence Partnership (2003) *Learning Mentor Training* (3rd edn). London: DfES.

Maslow, A. (1962) *Towards a Psychology of Being*. New York, NY: Nostrand.

Chapter 5

Partners in mathematical learning

Sue Cronin and Christine Bold

Our experience of working with teaching assistants who are supporting children learning mathematics leads us to believe that there are three crucial issues the classroom teacher must consider in order to ensure effective learning for pupils: communication, competence and confidence. All of these can be developed through, and in turn strengthen, a good working relationship between the teacher and teaching assistant.

Recent research reported by Lee (2002) suggests that learning is most effective when adults who are supporting children as learners are fully involved in lesson planning so that they understand the learning objectives of the lesson. There has to be an ongoing dialogue between the teacher and supporting adult to ensure that they share the same goals and have the same understanding of their pupils' needs (DfES, 2002). The communication between them needs to be a two-way process. While teachers have expertise in teaching and knowledge about what mathematics to teach, and can share ideas on the best ways to approach a particular topic, teaching assistants and other supporting adults, through their close pupil contact, will often develop intimate knowledge of pupils and understand how they think. Thus teaching assistants will often be in a position to inform teachers' understanding of their pupils' needs. It is important for effective learning by pupils that the adults who are supporting their learning are confident, competent and enthusiastic about the mathematics they are involved in helping those pupils to understand. This can be achieved largely through a good working relationship between the teacher and support assistant, which includes frequent discussion of the topics about to be taught, backed up, where possible, by training. Many teaching assistants have gained greater mathematical knowledge and understanding of mathematics through in-house training and training organized by LEA or Education Action Zones.

●●● Confidence

It is essential, not only that mathematics teachers should appreciate that teaching assistants and other supporting adults may not have the same confidence and enthusiasm for their subject that they have, but also that they should be proactive in trying to change this. In our work on training courses for teaching assistants across the range of primary and secondary schools, we have found that responses to the question 'What is mathematics?' often have a common theme, because their answers often have an emotional flavour. In other words, their responses are often about what mathematics *feels* like to them. For many people mathematics is a subject that invokes strong negative feelings, varying from dislike and frustration, to fear and panic. It is important to note that this is not the case with all; a minority are much more positive and express enjoyment, some often enjoying tackling number puzzles and problem-solving. For these assistants the issue of confidence in supporting learning in the subject may not be as significant, although feeling positive about a topic does not automatically mean that the adult will have the same level of confidence in explaining it to a child.

It is interesting to compare the mathematical mind maps produced by a significant number of teaching assistants and primary teacher trainees, with those produced by trainee secondary mathematics teachers embarking on a PGCE course. In answer to the question 'What is mathematics?' the majority of responses from teaching assistants are far more emotional than those from trainee, secondary mathematics teachers. Although the words 'fun' and 'feel-good factor' are used, the trainees put a greater emphasis on the nature of mathematics in terms of processes and skills, using words such as 'problem-solving' and 'language'. We point out to the secondary trainees the importance of their realizing that their perceptions of the subject, formed from their mathematical experiences, might differ considerably from those of most other adults, including many of the assistants they will be working with, and that it is very important to bear these differences in mind. Many primary trainees learn to overcome initial fears of the subject by building their pedagogical and subject knowledge. A confident primary teacher, with a strong knowledge of mathematical education, can build a productive working relationship with a teaching assistant. Not everyone has the same level of enthusiasm for maths, often because of a feeling of failure in the subject at some point.

We have found the mind-mapping exercise a very useful starting point for discussion of both colleagues' and students' attitudes to maths, as the answers are an indication of the mathematical experiences they have undergone. Many adults have a misplaced belief that they are no good at mathematics, when what they really mean is that they have experienced a failure in school-based mathematics. It would be easy to say that this was the result of poor teaching – we all know how easy it is to blame the teachers! But although some will undoubtedly have experienced some poor, uninspired mathematics teaching, the underlying reasons are usually far more complex.

Fraser and Honeyford (2000) explore the phenomenon of 'sum stress' experienced by some school children and give a list of typical reasons, which include past failures or a particularly bad experience in a lesson; parental attitudes; relationships with mathematics teachers; and physical problems such as dyspraxia and dyslexia. They cite research by Skemp (1986) which suggested that the underlying cause of 'sum stress' was rooted in the traditional methods used to teach, with the emphasis on rote learning rather than on understanding.

One or more of these factors may make a large contribution to the negative ways in which many teaching assistants respond to the subject. In fact this may be the case for some teachers who may similarly have had negative attitudes to their own abilities in mathematics as a result of these factors. Carvel (1999) quotes a primary schoolteacher recalling her own public humiliation in class for failing to understand a problem. This is often a common memory for adults who recall a childhood fear of failing in mathematics and suffering such a public humiliation. By discussing the origins of the teaching assistants' negative attitudes, teachers and teaching assistants themselves can start to redress the balance and develop greater confidence in their ability to cope with mathematics. We have found that teaching assistants appreciate the opportunity to consider their experiences at school – the ways in which they were taught mathematics – and that, when they do, they generally develop a greater openness and willingness to reconsider the subject in a new light. Their level of comfort and confidence with the idea of supporting children's learning in mathematics is usually increased, and this in turn can give a boost to their enthusiasm for the subject that will transmit to the children.

Shared planning and the opportunity to provide feedback, an issue raised at the beginning of the chapter, are often the key to building confidence. Another way to build teaching assistants' confidence is, as we have already said, for them to attend courses. Sometimes, unfortunately, this results in the teacher losing confidence in his or her own ability to manage and monitor the learning situation as the teaching assistant becomes both more confident, and more competent, in modifying the approaches he or she adopts to suit individual pupil's needs. In the story that follows, Dennis's experience provides an illustration of how minimal communication between support assistants and teachers with regard to mathematical planning can deny them the level of competence they need, if they are to address children's difficulties.

Scenario 1 – Dennis's experience

Dennis had worked for many years as a self-employed joiner and as a hobby he taught judo to children in local school-based clubs. His experiences with the children led him to consider changing his main occupation, so he took up a part-time position in a school as a support assistant in Years 4 and 5. He settled into the role well, but often found himself in the position of supporting children without the benefit of seeing the teachers' plans. In particular, when children struggled to complete the mathematics activities, Dennis lacked confidence in his ability to help them by breaking down the problem into an easier one. He tried to discuss this with one teacher who said that it was her job to decide the level of difficulty for the children, not his. Although he agreed with the teacher, he also felt inadequate in being able to support the children, and took steps to improve his knowledge of the mathematics curriculum by attending a relevant college course. He discovered that his 'gut feelings' about the need to break down the mathematics into easier steps had been correct, and he learned how to use the framework of the National Numeracy Strategy to identify the progression from one step to another.

Dennis proceeded to act on his newly found knowledge, turning it into expertise in the classroom, and the children with whom he worked had much more success as a result. The mentor in the school, however, expressed concerns to Dennis's college tutor that a teaching assistant was learning things that teachers need to know, and that he was using his initiative in tackling the children's difficulties. The tutor explained that teaching assistants often had responsibility for a lower-attaining group in mathematics, but without the knowledge needed to enable them to provide effective support. The course Dennis was attending provided that knowledge, and was in no way intended to undermine the teachers' expertise in the school. On the tutor's last contact with the school, she asked the headteacher how well Dennis, one of her most able students, had settled into the school and the headteacher's response was 'He's great, but we have to keep a tight rein on him'.

In this story Dennis took steps to build his level of confidence in relation to maths through an external course about mathematics, designed for teaching assistants, but it seemed that the staff in school might have felt threatened by this. There was evidently some discord between the teaching assistant role that Dennis and his college tutor perceived and that expected by the school. Communication in such a situation could be improved through shared planning time and open discussion about ways of teaching mathematics to lower attainers. If they open up the communication channels between them and Dennis, the teachers with whom he worked should become more confident that he was not trying to undermine them.

It is evident from our work with teaching assistants and primary trainees that some primary teachers, unfortunately, still lack the necessary confidence in teaching mathematics despite the recent National Numeracy Strategy intensive training and support. This is evident in the way the planning for the curriculum is often rigidly determined by the National Numeracy Strategy unit plans (2002) rather than the individual needs of the children. In primary schools, one can meet teaching assistants who are trying to support children in learning mathematics that they are not ready for, because they do not understand the previous steps of learning. Problems can arise in such situations because the teaching assistant does not have the knowledge to revisit these earlier steps with the child, especially if a teacher feels undermined by an assistant who decides the work is 'too difficult' for the child. Another problem in such situations can arise if a teaching assistant, believing he or she fully understands the problem, then uses methods to explain the mathematics which are 'tricks' to help the child finish the work, rather than methods and resources that help to develop the child's understanding of the underpinning mathemetical knowlege. This type of situation often arises where there is insufficient time for sharing planning and opportunity for the assistant to provide feedback, and also where the teacher himself or herself lacks confidence and mathematical knowledge. Having said this, in our experience there are now fewer instances of this type of occurrence than there were four years ago when the National Numeracy Strategy unit framework (DfEE, 1999) was launched.

●●● Competence

The issue of mathematical competence is often difficult to resolve. A teaching assistant who feels unsure is unlikely to operate with a high level of competence and conviction, regardless of his or her level of mathematical knowledge. So it is vital to consider the importance of confidence building, but this does not compensate for a lack of mathematical knowledge. If the supporting adult is, say, uncertain of the result if one divides seven by zero, wondering, for example, whether it is seven or zero when actually the correct answer is that it is mathematically undefined, he or she could inadvertently reinforce pupils' misconceptions. One way to avoid scenarios like this is to discuss common misconceptions at the start of the topic, drawing the supporting adult's attention to some of the potential pitfalls. Involving assistants in the initial planning process allows them to become aware of the areas to focus on with the pupils, and to consider how to address pupil errors and misconceptions. The confidence and competence factors are probably even more significant in the secondary school, where the level of mathematics at Key Stage 4 will often prove to be new territory and thus daunting for the supporting adult. One secondary school we know has adopted an interesting approach to this problem by taking steps to have some assistants sit in on GCSE classes to brush up their own knowledge with, in some cases, a view to the assistants taking the exams themselves in the future. This can result in some very positive benefits for pupils who have the opportunity to witness adults who are not only learning but valuing the experience. It provides the pupils with a different and very valuable perspective on learning.

Primary mathematics may not reach such an advanced level of mathematics but may present supporting adults with unfamiliar mathematical areas and strategies, which are similarly daunting. Certainly, with the introduction of the National Numeracy Strategy, mental methods of calculating such as 'partitioning' may be very different from the teaching assistants' own experience of learning mathematics. A familiar response to the first encounter with the new approaches to calculation is often an intake of breath, followed by 'that's not how we were taught'. Initially, adults may think that some of the 'new' methods, such as those involved in 'chunking' (subtracting multiples of the divisor) for division, are harder than using the algorithms they were taught. If you are an adult who managed to learn by rote how to complete a long division calculation, then the 'chunking' method might not seem to make much sense. It will take you longer, because you will not necessarily have the mental mathematics and estimation skills required for efficient 'chunking'. Once people become efficient at the 'chunking' method, however, the link with the method they learned as a child becomes evident, and the full advantages of chunking understood.

The National Numeracy Strategy methods help the child to keep a sense of the numbers and, in spirit the stategy is trying to avoid what Smith (1999) refers to as 'virtual' mathematics teaching – that is, teaching maths that relies on ritualized procedure rather than on understanding. The 'virtual mathematics teacher', in his opinion, which we support, fails the students by expecting them to learn without full understanding, relying on 'rituals' and 'rules' to supply the right answers. He cites reasons for this approach – for example, class management issues. After all, it is easier to say 'just learn this; it works – it will give you the answer!' than to explain the mathematics to a challenging class. In some cases, it is simply a case of history repeating itself, and the mathematics teachers' teaching a topic in exactly the same way as they themselves were taught. Whatever the reasons, the outcomes are less than satisfactory even for pupils who can remember the correct 'ritual'. If they do not understand why it works, the exercise is meaningless because attempts by subsequent teachers to make connections between different aspects of mathematics will fail. The pupil will experience feelings of dissatisfaction and a negative attitude to the subject is more likely to result. 'Virtual' mathematics teachers unintentionally pass on the concept of mathematics as an 'arbitrary collection of meaningless procedures' rather than a real understanding for the rich interconnections that form the subject.

Sharing with teaching assistants the importance of making mathematical connections with pupils is very important for maths teachers. In their final report on effective teaching of numeracy, Askew *et al.* (1997) identified the most successful teachers of numeracy as those who had a connectionist orientation to mathematics teaching. These teachers made explicit the links between different aspects of mathematics, and between maths and other subject areas whenever possible. They encouraged pupils to construct interconnected mental learning frameworks that allowed them to make sense of and interpret the world. New learning must 'connect' to previous learning, or it will be incomprehensible and dismissed. Vygotsky (1978) believed that pupils learn when they can recall what they have already learned, and then extend their existing mental maps to accommodate new learning; thus teachers and assistants need to ensure that the connections between old and new are explicit for pupils. Again, these connections should be considered when planning work and involving teaching assistants in the planning stage, as it can help them to become aware of links they should be reinforcing with the pupils. Recent research into learning and, in particular, accelerating learning by Smith (1999) and Hughes *et al.* (2000) highlights this as one of the first stages in the learning cycle; connecting previous learning to current understanding. Sharing this philosophy with teaching assistants is important and imitates the learning cycle itself. The teacher is sharing the 'big picture' with the assistant and ensuring that he or she understands not only what the teacher wants the pupil to learn, but also how and why he or she wants them to learn it.

Hughes uses the analogy of a jigsaw – the learner needs to see the complete jigsaw picture on the front of the box in order to make sense of how the individual pieces of the jigsaw fit together. It is just as important and relevant to share the methodology of learning with the assistant as it is with the pupils.

Teachers also ought to share knowledge of more recent developments in terms of learning styles and thinking skills with their teaching assistants. It is important for assistants to be aware not only of the pupils' preferred learning styles, but of their own learning styles, just as it is for the teacher. Just as the teacher is likely to transmit knowledge and skills predominantly in a way that matches with his or her preferred learning style so, too, is the assistant likely to have a dominant style, which may not match that of the pupils he or she is working with. Many secondary schools are now helping pupils to reflect on their personal learning styles–visual, auditory or kinaesthetic, through questionnaires and audits. Some have a colour code, and pupils record in their diaries which is their predominant style, so that teachers can ask pupils to show them their diaries and, at a glance, can see the range and proportions of visual, auditory and kinaesthetic learners in front of them.

Being aware of the preferences of the pupils they are working with allows the teacher to provide opportunities and resources that fit these preferred styles. However, we must recognize that pupils should not be exclusively limited to the one learning style, and there is a need to cover all learning styles to provide a variety of stimuli. In primary schools there has always been a greater use of practical and kinaesthetic approaches to learning and, particularly with the Numeracy Strategy, the variety of stimuli used in teaching mathematics has increased. There is a wealth of ideas and approaches to using equipment such as 100 squares, number fans, wipe boards, washing lines and blank counting sticks. The use of such resources is also increasing in secondary schools, particularly at Key Stage 3, and teaching assistants often use these to great effect with individual pupils or small groups to reinforce learning objectives.

A key element of successful teaching and learning is questioning. Assistants need to develop skills in questioning and discussing mathematics with pupils in order to support effective learning. For pupils to succeed they need to reflect on their mathematical understanding and be confident in their ability to tackle new problems using this understanding. They need to be able to plan and select the knowledge and skills required by the task in hand, and to reflect on and evaluate the results they obtain. Explicitly teaching thinking skills has a positive impact on the mathematical performances of low-attaining pupils. These pupils may require more help to develop these metacognitive skills; here the teaching assistant can help by facilitating them in discussing what they already know, and what they need to know to solve a problem. The teaching assistant can provide extra guidance as the pupil considers the best strategies to tackle a problem and can prompt him or her to talk through his or her planning, execution and evaluation of a task. Questions, which can prompt the pupils into the metacognitive process of thinking about their thinking, could include in the initial phase 'Do you understand what the teacher is asking you to do? What is the task/problem all about?' Low-attaining pupils often have misconceptions as to the task or problem they think they are undertaking, and discussion with a teaching assistant can help them to become clearer not only about the task but also about the best strategy for achieving success. Through directed discussion and focused questioning, assistants can lead pupils to a greater understanding of mathematics, particularly by asking them to explain how they have arrived at an answer. Facilitating pupils in articulating their thinking processes can reveal what the pupil knows not only to the adults concerned, but also to the pupils themselves. Often it is when they have to say out loud what they have done that they realize they have made a mistake or that they are just not sure of what they mean exactly. It is also possible to assess a pupil's grasp of a problem by the quality of the questions he or she asks; here again, assistants working one to one or with a small group can establish the expectation that pupils should join in and ask questions about their work, which they may be unwilling to do in front of the whole class.

Discussion and questioning are also essential if the pupils are to develop a grasp of the necessary mathematical vocabulary; here teaching assistants can help to familiarize pupils with the language of the subject by modelling. Pupils need to realize that talk is a valuable tool for thinking. Helping children to be able to talk mathematically about their ideas and to be able to discuss their work with fellow pupils is essential and requires a positive and supportive learning environment. However, the assistant needs to be facilitated in developing a certain level of competence in mathematics and pedagogical practices in order to capitalize fully on the learning experiences offered to the child through questioning and discussion. This is exemplified in the following scenario.

Scenario 2 – Marie's experience

Marie was a nursery nurse who had worked in the Reception department of the same school for 12 years. She was a well respected member of staff and the mentor in the school considered her a good candidate to progress to teacher training. Her words were 'She is doing the job now!' meaning that Marie had significant responsibilities for children's learning within the team. Based on the planning that the two Reception teachers shared with her each week, Marie organized the practical activities associated with topics in a specific area of the classroom. The children rotated around three different areas in the classroom over a period. In Marie's area she organized role play, baking, water play, sand play and a variety of art and craft activities.

When I saw Marie in her working environment, it was purely to share practice. I was not there in the role of assessor. Marie was engaged in a baking activity when I arrived and afterwards we discussed the language used in the activity and the potential to draw out the mathematical ideas in particular. Marie commented: 'I'm glad you have come in to talk to me because I would not have thought of deliberately introducing new language or mathematics.' She focused mostly on ensuring that children followed procedures and learned how to be hygienic in their handling of food. However, as I pointed out to her, she had indeed used mathematical language when counting out the measures of ingredients, and so we discussed how to involve the children more fully in the counting. We also discussed the idea of sequencing as an important concept in mathematics as well as in English, so in fact there was a strong element of mathematical development within the activity. Marie recognized that she needed to be more knowledgeable about how to capitalize on mathematical learning opportunities that arose.

As we extended our discussion about the planned areas of development for the rest of the morning, Marie related a story about the setting up of the role-play area. She had decided to focus on creating a small village shop, but the children's experience was of supermarkets. This created some interesting discussions about the size of the shop and the type of items they expected to be in it. She asked me how I would resolve the problem, without the opportunity for a visit to a shop. We discussed various options such as photographs and TV programmes that children would be familiar with, but more interesting was that Marie admitted to not realizing the full mathematical potential in such a role-play area. Her focus had been on the use of a till for handling money to buy and sell. On discussion with me, she realized the opportunities afforded for looking at shape and space, capacity, mass and time. Again, she recognized that although intuitively she was providing relevant and worthwhile experiences for the children, and managing these effectively, there were further opportunities for subject knowledge development that she had not previously considered.

We both came away from our discussions feeling that they had been fruitful.

Communication between the teachers and Marie was good and she had a clear role as a valued member of staff, but she still lacked some knowledge about mathematical ideas and where opportunities lay to address them in a range of contexts in which she worked with children. She also lacked the confidence to address this at planning meetings. She clearly benefited from more detailed discussion about the mathematical elements of her work with her tutor.

●●● Communication

It has become evident through our discussions of confidence and competency that communication is essential if teaching assistants are to develop either of these attributes. The three are inter-related and, unless communications between the teacher and teaching assistant are effective, there is little chance of improved confidence or competence in either party. Teachers who cultivate good relationships with their assistants, and who value their previous life experiences in addition to the learning they undertake on courses, find that they too benefit from increased confidence and competency. It has to be said that a whole-school approach to working with classroom assistants is best. The next scenario illustrates the potential benefits to be gained by reorganizing the workforce to aid communication.

Scenario 3 – A secondary solution

A secondary school with a high number of assistants (13) working with many low-attaining pupils had organized their assistants to work within departments, rather than being attached to one specific child. This seemed to be a successful approach to tackling some of the issues around communication, confidence and competence.

Two assistants chose to work in the maths department with all children who require extra support, with the exception of a few individual pupils who work with a particular assistant. By working all day supporting mathematics the assistants were increasing in their confidence and expertise in relation to numeracy strategies and mathematics far more quickly than they might have done had they been supporting mathematical learning only three or six lessons a week. The communication between the teachers and the assistants was now much stronger as they were not leaving the classroom at the end of the lesson with a pupil, having no time to stop and discuss progress. Time in between lessons can be valuable in terms of immediate feedback for the teacher on progress, behaviour or any other issue arising in the lesson. It may also be a chance to discuss the plan for the subsequent lesson and to remind the assistant of the key objectives and questions for pupils with whom he or she is working.

The assistants attended the departmental meetings and so felt part of the team, which was not a feeling engendered when they worked as general assistants supporting learning across all curriculum subjects. They also have regular short daily meetings with the special educational needs co-ordinator and other assistants to discuss all pupils they are working with, so that they can pick up any issues that may arise across the subjects.

The assistants in this school have expressed a preference for this curriculum-based organization of their work. The two numeracy assistants were happy to build up subject support expertise and felt they have stronger, closer communication and links with the staff in the department than they previously had with teaching colleagues. As general support assistants, they felt as if they were 'jacks of all trades and masters of none'. By working exclusively in mathematics they are now developing specific mathematical knowledge, understanding and skills, and feel that this is good in terms of their career development. The pupils benefit as the assistants become more familiar with the subject and have an increased understanding of how to support them with specific mathematical learning needs. The teaching staff also prefer the arrangement as they are happy to build up a closer relationship with assistants they are more frequently in contact with, and seem to be more willing to find time to discus their planning.

It seems, therefore, that in this particular example there are benefits all round for pupils, teachers and support staff in the whole-school reorganization, and this might be a very good model to follow.

●●● A fine balance

There is obviously a strong link between the opportunity to engage in quality communication about mathematics and mathematics teaching, and the confidence and competence of participants in mathematics teaching and support. Some teachers might still worry about the boundaries and how they balance the weight of responsibilities, as teaching assistants become more knowledgeable and capable in their jobs. Many teaching assistants aspire to higher levels of professional expertise, but do not necessarily want to become teachers. Understandably some teachers will feel threatened by the increased awareness and understanding of the mathematics curriculum among assistants, especially if their own understanding of mathematical concepts is insecure. We must keep a balance, with teachers retaining major responsibility for the whole situation, while deploying teaching assistants to work for the most effective learning in the class. At the same time, teachers must accept that teaching assistants will develop detailed knowledge about particular children and about specific approaches to supporting their learning that can only enhance learning for the whole class. Both must work together as a team communicating clearly, improving both confidence and competence in their working relationship.

●●● References

Askew, M., Rhodes, V,. Brown, M., William, D. and Johnson, D. (1997) *Effective Teachers of Numeracy: Final Report.* London: King's College.

Carvel, J. (1999) 'Teachers "too ashamed" to admit inability in Mathematics', *Guardian,* 2 September. Online at http/education.guardian.co.uk/news/story/0,78522,00.html

DfEE (1999) *The National Numeracy Strategy Framework for Teaching Mathematics - from Reception to Y6.* Cambridge: Cambridge University Press.

DfES (2002) *National Numeracy Stategy Unit Plans (Online)* (www.standards.dfes.gov.uk/numeracy/).

DfES (2003) *Working with Teaching Assistants in Secondary Schools* (video) London: DfES.

Fraser, H. and Honeyford, G. (2000) *Children, parents and teachers enjoying numeracy: numeracy hour success through collaboration.* London: David Fulton.

Hughes, M,. Desforges, C. and Mitchell, C. (2000) *Numeracy and Beyond.* Buckingham: Open University Press.

Lee, B. (2002) *Teaching Assistants in Schools – the current state of play.* Slough: NFER.

Smith, J. (1999) 'Virtual mathematics', *Mathematics Teaching,* 166: 14–15.

Tanner, H., Jones, S. and Davies, A. (2002) *Developing Numeracy in the Secondary School.* London: David Fulton.

Vygotsky, L.S. (1978) *The Collected Works of L.S. Vygotsky* (edited by Robert W. Rieber and Aarron S. Carton). New York, NY: Plenum Press.

●●● Chapter 6

Working with support to enhance the use of ICT

Sue Crowley and Mike Richardson

The use of computers and other ICT equipment in the classroom appears to be either loved or hated by the classroom teacher. Some see the computer as a boon to motivate and support children's learning, while others see it as 'that monster in the corner that won't work for me'. Whichever feeling you may have there is always the potential for an extra pair of hands and room for some more brainpower to work alongside the teacher in facilitating children's work in ICT. Ideally the teaching assistant working alongside children when they are engaging with computers should be positive about the use of ICT and have some experience of using computers. Whether this is your experience will, of course, depend on whether the assistant working with you has been employed due to a need in the school for enhanced ICT work or for other reasons.

●●● The unique place of ICT in the curriculum

ICT in the curriculum is unique: it is relatively new, it can be technical and off-putting, it is not a subject on its own and development across the curriculum requires knowledge of all other subjects. Primary teachers think about and teach across all subjects and must now regard ICT as a tool to take with them to support all subjects. Ofsted (2001) have noted that effective use of ICT across the curriculum is increasing but, still, good practice remains uncommon. A teacher working in partnership with an assistant could tip the balance. ICT is also unique in that it is modern and has 'street cred' with the children. Exciting, motivating and innovative ways of using ICT can support children's learning, and good programs (whether commercial or self-made) are helpful for children and give instant rewards. Therefore the teacher and classroom assistant working together should be able to create a good working environment for the children which embraces ICT in a natural way.

Loveless and Dore (2002) suggests that the unique features of ICT (interactivity, provisionality, capacity and speed) make a contribution to the teaching and learning process in that they motivate and interest children by engaging them in interaction, allowing them to change and amend work in progress and facilitate a variety of paces of working.

Interactivity

Interactivity allows the pupil to become more involved with his or her learning. A well designed program or Internet site can give immediate and dynamic feedback to a pupil's efforts at completing an activity such as matching pictures to the correct word. A child will go over an activity several times to gain a reward, such as a 'Well done' pop up from the program, and will also gain confidence as a result of getting feedback saying that he or she is right. This encourages the child to go on to the next level of work. There is the potential with Internet sites or CD-ROMs to enable a user to select hotspots (a kind of hyperlink) to a variety of other pages in order to find out information. A pupil interacting in this way with a computer is in control of his or her own learning. As Hardy (2000) emphazises, 'For pupils with special educational needs (SEN) there is a general acceptance of the value of interactivity, rather than pupils being passive recipients of knowledge'. Children with behavioural difficulties who are often unable to concentrate for more than ten minutes can become experts on all the varieties of hamsters, which can be found by selecting links from a CD-ROM. Self-esteem can grow even more when a mini-lesson is given to a group of peers. Children can also produce their own presentations with linking hotspots. This process encompasses design, research, decision-making, evaluating and presenting, and the authors have never yet met a child or adult who isn't proud of his or her accomplishments. A teaching assistant can also develop his or her skills in ICT alongside children in these activities if he or she is willing to see him or herself as a learner too. In the case of teaching assistants who are expert users of ICT, they will be invaluable in supporting the children in their learning.

Modelling or simulation programs that replicate a situation or circumstance in a virtual way rely on the interactivity feature of the computer, as the user makes decisions as to which route to take in the program. It may be discovering treasure in an Egyptian tomb or rescuing a princess from the wicked witch, but the experiences of trying out ideas and decision-making all lead to greater perseverance and an enhanced ability to solve problems. Of course, the route chosen through a problem/scenario may not always be a geographical one but may be a route chosen along a decision tree that leads to a range of possible solutions. By working closely with the teacher, an assistant can be involved in the creation of interactive resources and, in some cases, amending worksheets to include links to more recently produced activities. As this is a creative activity the assistant can bring his or her experience and development into the creative process in a natural and constructive way.

Provisionality

The provisionality of ICT is possibly most acknowledged for its versatility and use to the writer, who is able to use it to get ideas down quickly, knowing that the text can be edited in a variety of ways. Children must be shown how to make use of the various functions – cutting and pasting, copying, etc – that allow them to edit their written work, gradually shaping it into a finished product, rather than the 'editing facility'. After initial outline planning of their writing, they should be encouraged to write a draft straight on to the computer, with the intention of redrafting it, rather than 'typing up' a finished effort. This is an ideal opportunity to use a teaching assistant as a co-writer to help children to reflect and alter their writing composed on a word processor. They are far more likely to do this on a computer than by the pencil-and-paper method. Visual images, music and graphs can also be easily changed due to the provisionality feature of ICT. ICT creates a wonderful opportunity to experiment with colours on a picture or pattern without the paper becoming soggy and brown!

Capacity

ICT has the capacity to access and store vast amounts of information. A teacher is able to store all his or her planning, recording and worksheets electronically, and the teaching assistant is ideally placed to help organize and retrieve the information when needed, because this task is time-consuming and difficult to stay on top of without extra help or time off to do it. The reason it is done is because the planning can then be easily amended or updated without having to rewrite the whole document. This is helpful for the future as well, when a teacher may wish to amend a lesson to make it appropriate for a different group. Children have the opportunity to search an enormous amount of information from the Internet and CDs. Hardy (2000), writing about the use of ICT in relation to inclusion, points out the importance of ICT to pupils with a range of special needs: 'The capacity of CD-ROMs to store images, text, sound, movement and colour in digital form, and present them in multimedia interactive fashion are characteristics commonly quoted as likely to engage students with a whole range of behavioural and learning difficulties.' However, this in itself can produce difficulties, as there may be times when the amount of information is too daunting and the teacher and assistant need to help or structure the research for the child. An understanding of the information gained also needs to be organized by the teacher, as simply retrieving information does not automatically lead to knowledge and understanding.

Speed

The speed of the automatic functions of ICT enables children to concentrate on the task in hand and higher-order thinking and skills, while the technology carries out the reiterative processes. For instance, scientific inquiry may be interrupted when the children spend a great deal of time constructing a graph to represent their data; using ICT to analyse the data means that thinking about the investigation can be almost continuous.

●●● The role of the teaching assistant in suporting work in ICT

A teaching assistant could be very usefully employed working across the whole school with ICT, liaising closely with the ICT co-ordinator. This would be a great boon for the science co-ordinator, and we would imagine that many would welcome the idea. However, for the purposes of this chapter, we will assume that the assistant is designated to a class; many of the ideas, however, could easily be adapted for a whole-school situation.

ICT should support all subjects and should cover all types of ICT but, most importantly, it should be used appropriately and be planned into the curriculum and not used *ad hoc* or as a reward for quick work. While planning ICT work, the National Curriculum (NC) must be considered. However, the ICT NC essentially covers aspects of good practice in education, which must be covered through the medium of ICT.

It is important that both the teacher and the teaching assistant feel confident that they can support their children with ICT skills and have sufficient knowledge to be able to plan appropriate ICT into the curriculum for all abilities of children. A teacher should work together with the assistant in partnership to develop ICT capability for themselves and their pupils. If the assistant is fairly new to ICT and the teacher has some knowledge, then they should perhaps spend some concentrated time (e.g. an INSET morning or afternoon) going through the basics. It is also profitable to cover whatever ICT is planned for the term/year – it is far more productive spending some length of time in a calm atmosphere than attempting to instruct someone within a busy school day. If necessary, the teacher should arrange for the assistant to gain the equivalent of centrally funded training (New Opportunities Fund) in order to become proficient and capable with the children. Once an assistant is trained and has an enthusiasm for ICT, the amount he or she can do to support the teacher, and ultimately the children, is endless. Motivation is the key and, once motivated, there are many things an assistant can do to support the teaching that do not depend on a high level of technical skill, but are interesting and influential in children's development. The following are suggestions of work the teaching assistant could undertake.

●●● The invaluable support of the teaching assistant

Using features of word processors to support children's writing

The teaching assistant can produce professional and motivating worksheets by using a word processor. These worksheets are easily amended and can be saved for future classes. The main advantage of using a computer to write and store worksheets is the ease of differentiation; for example, a numeracy worksheet on spending money can be produced with the same illustrations of articles for sale but different prices for the differing abilities of the children.

Worksheets or files can also be produced for the children to use on the computer. By careful design, the children see what is needed and, often, there are opportunities to include supportive comments that can be removed on completion of the work. A blank, white screen with strange icons and menu words may be just as daunting to a child beginning a new piece of writing as a blank page and a pencil. This can be changed dramatically. First of all a new, chunky, child-friendly toolbar can be made. (Note: the following instructions may need adjusting depending on which version of Word you have installed.)

1 From the Tools menu, select 'Customize'.

2 In the Customize pane, select the Toolbars tab. This allows you to select which sets of icons you want to display.

3 To make a simple toolbar deselect all the standard toolbars and select New on the right-hand side of the Customize pane. Click OK.

4 Give the toolbar a name.

5 A small toolbar appears.

6 Drag the toolbar up to the Menu bar.

7 Select the Commands tab and drag an icon into your new toolbar. More icons can be added by dragging them from the commands menu. This toolbar will remain at the bottom of 'Choices' for future selection. Icons can be enlarged from the Options tab in the Customize pane. This method allows icons to be taught one at a time and prevents children 'experimenting' with icons.

Selecting the Format menu and then 'Background' or 'Theme' can change the background colour. This may seem more attractive to children and may actually be useful to dyslexic or visually impaired children. Some dyslexic children prefer a lilac background with black text, while some favour a yellow background with navy-blue text. Research carried out by a student at Liverpool Hope University College in 2003 reported that visually impaired children read more easily if the text was white on a red background.

Images from Clip Art or those found at Google can be inserted on to a blank page for young children. This may act as an incentive to writing as the printout will look professional. Several images could be placed on the page, enabling the child to select his or her preference and to delete the others. Obviously, older children can be taught how to insert and move their own pictures. Through the Format menu, Borders and shading, Page Border tab, an arty border can be placed on a page for the children (this will not work on a coloured background). This will also be more attractive than a blank page.

Writing frames can be made for all children or for certain children who need support. These could support the writing of book reviews, science investigations or any written work by giving open-ended questions or word cues. These frames are often best constructed within a table. Once a table is inserted (Table icon or Table menu), cells can be merged, and more cells, rows and columns inserted to suit your needs. Simply investigate the Table menu to see what can be done.

The spellchecker on word processors can help children with their spelling (providing the AutoCorrect is turned off) as children can look up the marked words in the computer dictionary or their own dictionaries. However, children are best supported through the use of *word banks*. Word banks can be used by the emergent writer through to all stages of education as the facilitator decides, possibly in consultation with the user, which words or phrases need to be entered into the word bank. The emergent writer may have all the words of a single sentence entered into the word bank for selecting to make his or her own first real sentence; the reluctant writer can have most of the words to be used in his or her writing in the word bank, with many attached to picture clues; and the young scientist could have all the technical vocabulary entered into the word bank as a reminder and for ease of spelling. The authors have experienced a change in the demeanour of children of all ages and abilities when writing with the support of a word bank. It became such a joy to write for one male, 9-year-old reluctant writer when using an overlay board programmed with relevant words who had to be prised off the computer at the end of the day having been writing virtually all session. This was a complete change from his usual rush to be first out of the door. His enthusiasm remained the next day when he saw his writing had pride of place on the display board, and the self-esteem he gained transferred to other lessons whether using a computer or not. The teacher can often predict what words the children will need for their writing, particularly if based on a particular ongoing topic, and thus give the teaching assistant time to make word banks. Some may need to be adapted or made on the spur of the moment, but even this should not be too difficult for the teaching assistant and is so rewarding it becomes a worthwhile activity.

Using the Internet

The Internet is so vast that no one person can ever know all the best sites for his or her purpose and a teacher may be far too busy teaching to be able to spend time browsing. However, the teaching assistant could be invaluable in this respect if he or she is given time every so often to search for suitable sites or information. The search may be for background information for teaching, for instance by using the key words 'Florence Nightingale' (use speech marks if you want the search engine to find sites where the words always come together). From this search the Florence Nightingale museum can be found (www. florence-nightingale.co.uk) which contains some good illustrations for printing out as well as informative text. The children can then compare a nurse's uniform of today with that of Florence's time. Some informative sites written for children can be printed out and made into an interactive book as an extra resource for the classroom when a computer is not available. Pages need to be numbered so that, instead of selecting a link, the teacher writes the appropriate page number next to the wording of the link.

The teaching assistant will be able to search for suitable sites for children to gain information about the current topic. If the objective of the lesson is to research a subject and to find particular information, you do not want the children searching aimlessly for the majority of the lesson. If the lesson objective is for the children to learn how to search, then that is a different matter. Once a suitable site has been found it can either be bookmarked or an interactive worksheet can be made which asks questions and leads the pupil straight to the site.

An interactive worksheet can be prepared in Word, Excel and in some children's word processors, such as Textease. Once you have chosen the site:

1   Load a Word page.

2   Think about having a coloured background or a theme from the Format menu.

3   Decide whether you want the children to place their writing on a separate new page (i.e. make a copy of your original document) or to delete the instructions on your page, to write on it and save under their own name (in which case you will have to save your original document as a template).

4   Note the exact web page you want to send the children to, including http://

5   Write a linking word or phrase on your document. Highlight the words. Select the Insert Hyperlink icon or go to the Insert menu and select Hyperlink.

6   Ensure the top-left hand tab is highlighted (Existing File or Web Page), then type the web address into the appropriate box (you could copy the web address then use Ctrl + V to paste it in).

7 Save your page and try the link.

8 Write appropriate questions for the children on the page.

Just as there is a vast amount of information out there, there are also hundreds of sites of children's activities, and the teaching assistant needs to sort out the better ones or the ones that are most appropriate for some or all of the children. The best advice is to stick to those produced by well-known organizations such as the BBC (www.bbc.co.uk/schools) or the government's Grid Club (www.gridclub.com), but there are many other worthwhile activity sites. They can be used to reinforce ongoing work or as an added extra.

One of the most exciting features of the Internet for children is the email feature. It gives children a real purpose for writing and they are more likely to get quick feedback. The drawback of email is that, depending on how it is organized, it may be necessary for someone to vet the incoming mail before the children read it; this could be a task for the teaching assistant. In most cases, however, this will not be necessary as the teacher can organize whom the children are writing to (a class of children in another location, for instance). Even very young children can use email with adult help. One idea may be for a Reception class to draw self-portraits in Paint (an almost universal program found in the Accessories of Windows computers). These pictures can then be attached to an email to send to another class. Older children can compare localities, discuss a topic, begin to learn a new language or ask an expert about their current topic. A project could even be set up whereby the children are emailing the teaching assistant under the guise of an author or a councillor to argue about the new road that is planned to go through the children's park!

Control and monitoring

Control and monitoring are the least used aspects of ICT in schools. Ofsted (2002) report that:

> *Very few schools, for example, give pupils satisfactory access to control technology, to data-logging or to modelling on the computer. As a result, most schools fail to extend pupils' natural progression from early software that helps them to understand cause and effect. Similarly, there are too few opportunities to develop increasingly complex mathematical skills within a practical and engaging context.*

One of the reasons that it is not such a popular activity may be that the equipment for control and monitoring is relatively expensive, and becoming familiar with the equipment and completing projects with the children are time consuming. The teaching assistant could be an invaluable help in this area of ICT.

Whereas monitoring has a place in the science or geography curriculum, control can either have the context of a topic or may be a topic in its own right. Programmable toys, such as the Roamer, can be used with early years children to estimate numbers and length or can be dressed up as a character from a book or object from the current topic and 'instructed' to go on a journey (e.g. Postman Pat delivering letters to houses). They can also be employed with older children using more complex instructions, which are often LOGO related. The activity may be one set by the teacher (such as emulating an ice-cream van travelling down roads, stopping and playing a tune) or may be a problem set by the children themselves in discussion with the teacher/teaching assistant.

Control technology involves model-making or the use of pre-made models with lights, buzzers, motors and sensors that are put on and off by programming a computer connected to a control box. The instructions given to the computer to control the models can range from simple turning on and off a switch to complex instructions that involve *if, then* and *until* commands (e.g. when light intensity is less than 20 then switch on light). These activities are valuable to a pupil's development as they enable children to understand how everyday devices work and also to think how they could work more effectively. They encourage logical thinking, problem-solving, perseverance and collaborative work. Through research, Stephenson (1997) has found that 'Children engaging in these kind of activities generally show a very positive attitude and are often more willing to take on the challenge of independent problem solving using control IT than they would be in more "traditional" contexts'.

Monitoring involves computer-controlled monitoring or measuring of light, heat or sound. As with control technology, it may be initially teacher intensive to set up, run and teach. Therefore both this and control are ideal tasks for an interested and able teaching assistant.

Presentation programmes

There is a lot of scope for the classroom assistant to contribute to the preparation of presentation materials when children wish to present their ideas. Word banks and phrases can be prepared in advance, and there is good software available to facilitate this. Even if the software isn't available it is still possible to use features within Microsoft Office to construct your own. By preparing documents as templates the ideas can be supported in a way that is in keeping with much of the good practice that already takes place. Paper templates for children can be used to present their findings, but having them stored as documents on a computer gives teachers several options. They can use them interactively with a whiteboard, on individual computers to support pairs of children or groups, on a network server to support lessons in a computer suite, or for printing out for use in the traditional way. These templates, often referred to as writing frames, can be dropped on to Notepad or Notebook software, giving additional interactivity tools within presentations with an interactive whiteboard.

As it may be cumbersome to have several paper examples to show to children, PowerPoint or other presentational software can make it possible to have several examples to show without difficulty. This is where ICT supports and enhances what the teacher wants to do, providing a richer pool of resources that can be dipped into. Many children hate the idea of constructing their work out of thin air, as it were, and this method of providing a worked example or a possible way of working allows them to develop their skills knowing they are being led or guided down a known path to success. Some simple presentations can be made in PowerPoint with animations already selected, and the decision is in the child's hands as to whether to retain them, modify them or substitute new ones.

Our experience has been that creating support materials is best done as part of a team and, in the school situation, this would be made up from teachers and the classroom assistants assigned to a year group. This reduces the burden upon individuals, and the synthesis of materials from a group is often of higher quality than from a single person. It is important not to try to do too much. If one resource is made for literacy and numeracy, for example each half-term, you soon build up a rich bank of ideas. Of course, the DfES has itself done much in the literacy and numeracy areas so it may be expedient to concentrate on the other areas of the curriculum. Work that spans the curriculum area boundaries is particularly effective and reflects the real world. This was borne out when we asked students with little or no experience of ICT resource making to provide materials that would enhance learning in other subjects. Once they had been shown some simple ideas (such as turning off the Automatic Advance feature in PowerPoint or using hyperlinks to move through documents), the results were amazing. More to the point, the buzz of excitement in creating things that were directly of use in the classroom boosted their confidence as ICT users.

Buttons that are used with hyperlinks can themselves make it possible to create documents that have choices within them. This enables children to construct their own route through the learning maze without fear – the possibilities of failures being limited in their power to cause loss of confidence while still being able to be valuable lessons. Different levels of support can be added at the discretion of the team. Mouse-over buttons (where the link operates when the cursor is on the link) enable actions and can be good where children find co-ordinating the click with the position of the cursor difficult. The team will need to work together to ensure that the skills and abilities within it are complementary so that this can happen naturally.

It is really a small step to go from this approach in PowerPoint and other presentation software to doing similar things with spreadsheets. As long as the spreadsheet allows the placement of hyperlinks and buttons, there are many ways they can be used to support learning. They are essentially designed with the ability to show what happens in 'what if?' scenarios. This enables children to explore, experiment, follow up and see what happens when they create hypothetical situations.

One of the author's children was highly motivated by this kind of activity when looking at a commercial software game called 'Rollercoaster' where a theme park could be designed and modelled. This idea of using a scenario to explore the effect of different variables is common in many games. Another on the Internet models a child's lemonade stall, the aim of the game being to sell as much, given weather conditions that vary and the costs of the ingredients. In fact, children are being given the chance to role play, which is a long-established tool in the primary teacher's toolbox.

Spreadsheets – graphing, number squares and formulae

Spreadsheets can be a useful tool in the class teacher's and teaching assistant's toolbox, but their chief usefulness in children's learning results from the way in which their more advanced features enable teachers to set up dynamic learning situations. This is due to the fact that a spreadsheet usually processes the numbers that are entered into it to model a situation or event. Children can even use these modelling features to experiment with numbers to see what happens when certain mathematical operations are performed singularly or in combination with other operations. Specific mathematical patterns can be explored, and simple data-handling operations are made less of chore because the processes can be easily repeated for sets of data. For example, the repeated addition of 2 to a number is easily explored and therefore multiplication by 2. One hundred squares are easy to create using AutoFill in Excel. Pattern is then easy to highlight using the Fill tool to 'colour in' the cells with multiples of 2.

Although some of the features are quite sophisticated in commercial spreadsheets, the look of the spreadsheet needn't be commercial in any way. You can change the way a spreadsheet appears to the child using the Formatting tools in the software. Of course, some of the primary spreadsheet software has taken these features away, but the software can still be used to model situations such as a simple pocket-money exercise: 'You have 50p, but how would you like to spend it so that you have 10p change.' The options can be on the spreadsheet in pictorial form with prices. The child has space to write his or her shopping list and can total it up. This kind of open question that invites investigation is often lacking, yet it rehearses all the skills required by closed questioning. In this way the child learns in situations that are closer to reality than add 24p, 13p and 5p.

It is also possible to hide the formulae in some spreadsheets by creating formulae on a work area that are then formatted to be invisible (highlight the columns you wish to hide; click on Format then, Column and select Hide). Other methods include selecting options that remove the formula bar. However, hiding formulae and the Formula bar and scroll bar can also hide some cells. The point is that these are features that involve a degree of lateral thought. By starting with the problem 'Children can see the answer', the spreadsheet designer must then think about how to prevent this. The more you look at the features of a spreadsheet and use them, the more you will think of ways you can use a feature to good effect. There are plenty of examples of spreadsheets used in this fashion on the Internet. Try a search on www.google.co.uk using 'spreadsheet modelling', or look at http://www.devon.gov.uk/dcs/ict/models/index.html for some examples of what can be done for Key Stage 2 children. However, other people's ideas are not always suitable for you, we recommend that you should try to model a simple idea and develop it from there.

Figure 6.1 is an example from Excel.

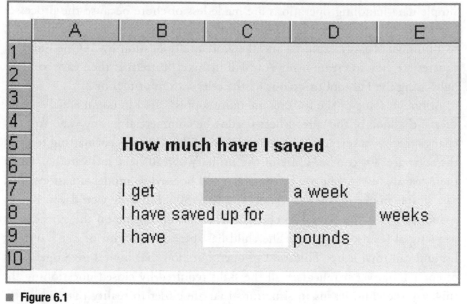

■ **Figure 6.1**
An Excel spreadsheet
Source: Figure source here the quick brown fox jumped over the lazy dog all day long.

In cell C7 and D8 the child can enter a number. The formula should be written in cell C9. Format cells C7 and D8 as unlocked:

1 Highlight C7: D8 and select Format, then Cells, Protection and uncheck the box next to Locked.

2 Choose Tools, Protection, Protect sheet.

3 Do not select a password.

4 The only cells the child can enter numbers in are C7 and D8.

The child can experiment to see how many weeks it takes to save any amount.

●●● ICT and professional development

There are a number of factors to consider when using ICT for teachers' and teaching assistants' professional development. There is the use of ICT to support the presentation of documents in things such as a CV or letter of application. ICT may also be used when collaborating in the production of materials for other staff in the school, for outside agencies (including the LEA and Ofsted) or for communicating with parents and governors. The tools for collaboration are often found as Options in the software. For example, the Reviewing toolbar in Microsoft Word has shortcut buttons that allow you to add comments to a text and to track changes in a document. Other tools include the use of email and, in some cases, a learning or collaboration environment sometimes referred to as a virtual learning environment (VLE) or a managed learning environment (MLE). The last two are not used in many schools at present but the trend is such that they need to be mentioned. If your school uses one, training from a member of staff in the school is vitally important. Email remains the main tool for collaboration, so it is important to know about how to attach a file to an email and also the importance of working in compatible versions of the document. It is also important to make sure that documents created in school can be opened at home if preparation is to take place on a computer at home. Some site licences allow for this, but it is important, as an example, to check that when working on a Textease document (Textease is a primary software package) that Textease is installed on the off-site machine you wish to work on. Once these skills are part of the team's array of skills there is a host of working arrangements that can enhance the performance of individuals, be they children or staff. Templates can be created for many administration documents, and the administration team at the school is often already engaged in making these for the staff to use. From the teacher's point of view it is important to make sure that classroom assistants have access to courses that teachers enjoy, particularly in the application of software to learning situations in the classroom and school.

●●● Conclusion

ICT has provided new and exciting ways of working. The 'communication' in the now-accepted title for the subject hints that it is a way of working, of enhancing communication. If we try to communicate over the telephone, for example, we have many advantages over communicating through the written word. Tone of voice and inflection will lend support to the meaning of what we have to say. We have all written messages to people that ended up being misunderstood, and some have disastrous consequences. We look back on these disasters and say 'but if only you had heard what I meant'. With the frenetic changes in communication we can not only communicate tone and inflection but also facial expressions, gesture and supporting illustrations that are themselves animated. These additions to our communication enhance and enlighten.

What we have also discovered is that we have preferences in the ways in which we communicate, which can even extend to our choice of language if that is part of our repertoire. Gardner's multiple intelligences theory (1983) states that for the learner it is important that he or she retains some choice over the way he or she receives information. This situation will mean that those imparting information have a great responsibility to make it as accessible to as many as possible if they want to communicate effectively. Until recently that was too difficult a task for many but now, through ICT, skills and tools to manage the process are available to all.

Software began as quite a logical mechanical method of communicating (for example, the earlier forms of computer language were quite mathematical) but, as skills developed, ways were discovered to develop more intuitive programs that used switches and buttons, hidden behind icons, that made the use of the software more accessible to those wishing to use the tool to communicate.

So now we have software that is accessible and intuitive to use. It requires training but is sophisticated enough to contain guides as to its use, whether it is software to communicate a budget or one that helps you display something of your feelings in a graphical manner (for example, an e-birthday card). The point is that communication is a deep-rooted activity in the heart of individuals as we are very social beings.

This chapter has examined how teaching assistants can help to put ICT at the centre of supporting children to learn and has presented the kind of support children need to do this. Communicating in multi-sensory ways will enhance learning. As well as encouraging their use, teachers and assistants need to ensure that their use is suited to the purpose.

●●● References

Gardner, H. (1983) *Frames of Mind: The Theory of Multiple Intelligences*. New York, NY: Basic Books.

Hardy, C. (2000) *Information and Communications for All*. London: David Fulton.

Loveless, A. and Dore, B. (2002) *ICT in the Primary School*. Buckingham: Open University Press.

Ofsted (2001) *ICT in Schools: The Impact of Government Initiatives – an Interim Report.*
    London: Ofsted.
Ofsted (2002) *ICT in Schools: The Impact of Government Initiatives on Pupils' Achievement.*
    London: Ofsted.
Stephenson, P. (1997) 'Children's learning using control information technology', in
    A. McFarlane, (ed.) *Information Technology and Authentic Learning.* London: Routledge.

●●● **Chapter 7**

The Teacher and the Nursery Nurse: building the partnership

Ann-Marie Jones

●●● Introduction

Teachers and nursery nurses often work closely together with children from 3 to 8 years of age in infant schools. Their training is different and yet their roles may appear to be very similar. In nursery class settings in particular, it is often difficult for a visitor to tell which of them is the teacher, especially when the nursery is running smoothly and the staff are working in close partnership.

Clearly their responsibilities are different and this is reflected in their pay and their status. Yet at the same time they must both carry out many of the same duties, such as providing age-appropriate activities, observing and assessing the children, recognizing when a child needs support and ensuring the children's physical safety and emotional security. They may also share some decisions and a certain amount of the planning and preparation.

If the responsibilities of both teachers and nursery nurses are carefully defined, then does the quality of their relationship matter? I would argue that careful definition is of major significance both for the staff themselves and for the children. Recently, in the perceptions of early years professionals working with children with disabilities, a sense of teamwork and 'common purpose' was identified to me as the most significant factor in assisting staff to carry out their duties effectively. Teamwork and a common purpose can also reduce anxiety, help confirm or change opinions about the children's needs, and reduce the burden of planning and assessment, making each day more satisfying and less stressful for both teachers and the nursery nurses. Where such teamwork does not exist, there is likely to be instead an air of tension, an unwillingness to be creative and a palpable lack of job satisfaction.

From the children's point of view there are multiple benefits to be gained from a successful partnership between the adults who hold the power to make the day happy and secure, fruitful and stimulating, or to let the tensions between them create an atmosphere of uncertainty and blame. Good ideas can become great when two informed professionals discuss and refine them. Everyday matters can become interesting again when they are shared, for instance, devising new opportunities for indoor physical exercise during the winter months or new ways to bring music into the daily plans. Motivation and energy will improve when each person feels valued and supported.

Bruce (1997: 168) emphasized the need for a partnership between the teacher and the nursery nurse wherein 'it should not be possible to say who is the stronger'. Similarly, Abbott and Moylett (1999: 180) contend that recent government initiatives concerning early years issues 'require something more than benign co-operation across existing professions'. Such professional relationships will demand respect for each other's knowledge and contributions. The aim of this chapter is to explore how this may be achieved, using characters created from my conversations with many teachers and nursery nurses over a number of years. I have been involved with training programmes for both professions and have used the thoughts and reflections of students and colleagues as the basis of the characters in this fictional setting. Regular visits to Nurseries, Nursery classes and Primary schools have provided material, as did my Master's thesis concerning perceptions of disability among early years professionals. Informal interviews with newly qualified teachers have also been used. The chapter will conclude with an overview of some principles of effective partnership between nursery nurses and teachers.

●●● The setting: Treetops Infant School

This is a primary school close to the centre of a city.

●●● The characters

Jan: the nursery nurse/early years practitioner

Jan is 30 years old and has been qualified for ten years. She has two children of her own aged 5 and 7 years and is confident about recognizing and meeting children's needs. Jan has been in this post for three years now. She found the first two years quite difficult as the teacher, Marianne, had been in the nursery for a long time and had become resistant to any further change. Jan had been informed kindly but firmly that no new approaches were needed, that the nursery was running very happily just as it was. She had wanted to try out regular changes to the home corner theme, and to put in place some early literacy strategies she had heard of during a course. But in the event she found that hers was not a significant voice in the school. In fact there had been several occasions when she had not been invited to staff meetings, being told they were mostly about the curriculum so she didn't need to trouble herself to stay after school. This had left her feeling marginalized and unimportant. She has now settled for doing her job to the best of her capacity, but without striving for the innovative or risking new ways. She has worked with a succession of supply teachers in the nursery for the past year, since Marianne took early retirement, and has found that she needs to put all her effort into just keeping everything running smoothly for the children.

Vicky: the nursery teacher

Vicky is 24 years old and newly qualified; this is her first job. She worked in an office for more than a year before deciding she would die of boredom if she stayed there and so she applied for teacher training. Her commitment is total: she has worked hard for four years to gain her qualification and her training has taken her to quite a cross-section of schools. She has a sensitive nature and has already realized that the quality of the relationships between staff can be one of the most significant factors in a school's success. She has so far worked with few nursery nurses and knows a little about their training.

Vicky is full of enthusiasm to put into practice all the theory she has learned and to discard some of the less successful practice she has witnessed! She is very much aware of the value of promoting children's independence to help them achieve their individual best and to avoid the trap of turning out 'clones' of well behaved 4-and 5-year-olds for Reception class. She visited the nursery briefly at her interview and knows that the nursery nurse is a little older than she is, but believes that this should not be a barrier. She has not been able to meet up again with Jan. She called in during the summer holidays to get the feel of the Nursery and see the resources, but Jan was elsewhere and did not join Vicky; then they were both away on holiday. During the summer she has been planning activities for her first nursery group.

Carol: the headteacher

Carol has been in the school for four years. She has had some difficulty taking the school ethos forward from a position where very little trust existed in the leadership after so many changes of headteacher in the preceding years. She has tried to create a much more positive approach where staff work together so that preparation for Ofsted, or having a mixed Year 1/Year 2 class, is seen as an opportunity to share ideas.

Sara: the student mentor

Sara is a Reception teacher and has been in post for nine years. She has seen the school go through considerable upheavals as one head succeeded another, each stamping his or her individual style without always realizing the strain it was causing the staff. She has worked with many lecturers from the local FE college, as the school regularly takes nursery nurse students, and from the university as part of the teacher training programme.

She is well aware of the difficulties Jan faced with the former nursery teacher, but felt unable to intervene at the time. However, since Marianne left a year ago, she has made a point of befriending Jan and discussing mentoring and training issues with her. She has a good understanding of the differences between nursery nurse and teacher training.

●●● Treetops Infant School

Term 1

Day 1: 8.00am

Vicky arrives for her first day at the school. She only returned from her holiday abroad last night (arranged before she gained this post) and so was unable to attend Friday's staff meeting. She enters the nursery class, which is carefully arranged for the morning session: tables are well spaced with small construction activities on some, drawing and drawing materials on others:

> *JAN: Good morning! I'm Jan - it seems ages since we met, doesn't it? It's good to have you here.* (I'd forgotten she looked so young! I hope she's up to this.)

VICKY: Hi! It's good to see you again, too. I'm just sorry we couldn't get together before, but anyway I'm here now and I'm so glad to be working with someone who knows the Nursery set-up and routine.(She's most probably thinking she'll have to do EVERYTHING and she looks so confident. Help!)

JAN: Well shall we just set out the jigsaws and then we're ready to let the children in?

VICKY: Do you always set up all the activities before the children come in? (I'm not sure I want to do it this way – at least not every day.)

JAN: That's how we've done things in the three years I've been here. (Here we go – trying to change things already!)

VICKY: Well, OK, I can see other activities are already out on the tables, so we might as well put out the jigsaws as well. (I've put my foot in it good style judging by her face. This could be even worse than I thought. Oh well! I'll just have to do my best.)

Day 2
During the next day the tensions continue to develop as Vicky asked questions about the Nursery routine and Jan, being busy, gave only brief answers.

Day 3
At the end of the morning, the headteacher, Carol, walks into the nursery to see how everything is going and observes this scene. Jan is chatting with parents as she hands over the children, keeping a watchful eye on the others at the same time. Before Vicky can cross the room, Jan has spotted Tom (aged 4 years) about to climb on to a window seat to look out of the window. Jan interrupts her own conversation to shout across a warning to Tom; Vicky stops mid-way across the room, then carries on over to Tom and takes him to find a book to distract him until his parents arrive. Meanwhile a fight has developed between two small girls, and one of them starts to scream in pain after being slapped across the face by the other, just as their mums arrive. Jan glares across at Vicky as she goes to calm the situation.

Day 4
Vicky is a little anxious about a repeat of yesterday's events and suggests that she should greet the parents at home time while Jan sees to the children:

JAN: Why can't we just share the task – it shouldn't be a problem.

VICKY: I find I'm not sure just what I'm supposed to be doing and I think it might be more straightforward to concentrate on either watching the children or speaking to the parents.

JAN: Well if that's what you want to do, but I can't see the need myself – if we're working together properly.

Day 5
Despite the problems so far, Vicky wanted to try to remain positive:

VICKY: Jan, I'm impressed with the way snack-time works so well: it can be difficult, can't it, if the children just want to carry on with what they're doing and you have to drag them away?

JAN: Well – it's my belief that they're far too young to have to remember to go over and collect their drinks themselves and there's the extra advantage that, when you bring them together, they can learn a few social skills, chat together and maybe sing a song to help them bond. [While she was talking, she has raised her eyebrows at two children who were squirting milk, scooped up another who had fallen off his chair, and generally kept a watchful eye everywhere.]

VICKY: But what about the children who maybe aren't ready for a snack or a drink and have to try and force it down – isn't that a problem sometimes?

JAN: I find it's just a case of getting them into the habit and mid-morning is usually about right. (What more proof does she need than what she's just seen?)

VICKY: I see what you mean-but I wonder if there could be advantages to having them collect drinks, pick up name cards, etc., to help prepare them for Reception. (Surely there needs to be some support for them becoming more self-directing?)

Week 2
Vicky is getting to know the children now but feels that the situation is little improved on last week.

Wednesday
Jan meets Sara at lunchtime:

SARA: So – how's it going?

JAN [with a slight grimace]: Well it could be worse I suppose. I just feel that she's watching my every move and waiting for something to pounce on.

SARA: Why should she do that, Jan – are you sure she's not just trying to learn?

JAN: Oh [sighing], maybe you're right. It's just she asks a question and then when I answer she hardly comments. On Monday, for instance, I was seeing the children out at mid-day and she was even less help than the average student nursery nurse would be – standing on the other side of the room and looking at me. Then when there was a problem she didn't notice in time and I had to sort it!

SARA: Hmm! Could it be that she's a bit scared to do anything? The thing is – you look so confident, you know each child's name and recognize the parents too.

JAN: Well, wouldn't it be more sensible for her just to ask me? The supply teachers I've worked with for the past year were only too keen to ask or to leave it to me!

SARA: Yes, but that's different, isn't it? They're not going to stay long and if you don't think much of their classroom skills, well – they may never see you again! Vicky's here for good and needs to get it right from the start.

JAN: You could be right, but she also needs to realize that things are done the way they are for a reason, not just at my whim!

Friday 3.30 pm

Vicky goes to see Carol, the headteacher:

CAROL: How's it going, Vicky? I couldn't help noticing you looked a little 'out of things' the other morning. Was I right?

VICKY: Yes, you were, although I hadn't realized it was obvious!

CAROL: It wasn't obvious at all: it was just that I was watching carefully and wanted to ask you how you were feeling.

VICKY: That's a relief! I thought perhaps I was being summoned to explain my slow start at picking up the Nursery reins.

CAROL: What makes you think it's a slow start? Did you expect to just walk in and go from zero to sixty miles per hour in a few weeks?

VICKY: No, no of course not, but I did think I should have quickly communicated a sense of authority to run the nursery successfully.

CAROL: OK – well that's interesting. I see where you're coming from. From among the teachers you have worked with, can you identify qualities that made them authoritative?

VICKY: That's a difficult question (she's thinking of some teachers who possessed very few such qualities!). *Probably those who impressed me the most were the ones who really welcomed me, even though I was only a student, who had time to explain things and made me feel I could contribute.*

CAROL: I know what you mean. So if we were to consider what it was about such a teacher, would you say it was knowing exactly what she was doing, being open to new ideas, having a sense of humour?

VICKY: All of those things. It was so different in some settings where the teacher was for ever shouting to gain attention. The children seemed to do a lot of shouting too, often quarrelling and being unco-operative. I suppose those teachers believed they were showing their authority that way, but in fact...

CAROL: Interesting isn't it, when you think about how differently they would work with other members of staff, nursery nurses for instance. I think it might help you to know that Jan didn't have the easiest of times with the previous Nursery teacher and then came a year of supply teachers.

VICKY: I see. Well I've always imagined working as partners rather than my issuing orders and the nursery nurse following them.

CAROL [rather briskly]: Good, I'm very glad to hear that – it was one of the reasons you got the job rather than the other candidates, so I'd be disappointed to hear otherwise!

VICKY: (That's me with my foot in it again!) *Jan has suggested meeting soon, with Sara as well. So perhaps we can sort out a few points.*

CAROL: Great – let me know how it goes.

Vicky leaves the room feeling that she understands Jan somewhat better but not at all sure that the head realizes the extent of Jan's reluctance to sit and discuss matters face to face. How to set up a partnership with a reluctant partner? That was going to be some challenge!

Vicky thought about the situation overnight and then decided to try to put the matter to the back of her mind, to take each day as it came and get on with her job. Thus she responded as she did the next afternoon. She asked the children to hand around a plate of the biscuits they had just baked, to take one each and pass it on. The plate was about half-way round when one child let it tilt and a few biscuits fell to the floor. Jan immediately took over and asked Kate, one of the oldest in the group, to carry the plate to each child in turn. She gave Vicky a reproving look and declared 'They're simply not ready for this yet and now someone goes without a biscuit!' Vicky just shrugged and looked away. What was the point of arguing or trying to defend her position?

Week 4

When eventually the promised meeting with Sara took place, Vicky said very little. As she listened to the information about the planned nursery curriculum for the term she found herself largely in agreement with the themes chosen. She wanted to ask about how they could encourage the children's independence more, as she was concerned they were starting to become very compliant, and did little without reference to the adults present. This was not the situation she wanted in her nursery. If only she really felt it was her nursery!

However, Vicky had made a few points that struck Sara as interesting. Since Sara had never worked in the nursery, she tended to accept Jan's views on most things. Sara decided to mention her thoughts to Jan after a few days, but sensed it would be as well to refer only in passing to Vicky's views; this approach made her uneasy but she was thinking long term and trying to avoid possible conflict. While she was beginning to feel some sympathy for Vicky, it was also the case that Jan was a close friend, as well as a colleague, and Sara recognized that she needed support more than advice at present. She had some success with this tactic and felt at the next planning meeting that there was a little more sharing of views and more listening. But there was still tension between Jan and Vicky, with Vicky wearily justifying her position and Jan reluctantly agreeing to accept it. A particular issue was that of seeing parents. She resolved to tackle the issue after half-term.

Week 7: the next planning meeting

VICKY I would really like to start offering parents proper appointments when they want to see us, so they at least have 10 or 15 minutes and we can sort out problems properly.

JAN [sounding exasperated]: How on earth are we going to find time to do that? Sometimes there can be four parents and I think a quick word with each to reassure them is best.

VICKY: But often it's the same people coming back. Maybe the problem was never really solved?

JAN: I don't agree. I think it's more to do with how we respond to them.

Sara could see value in both approaches, since both had the parents' best interests at heart, and she tried to offer this as a way forward. But in the end an uneasy compromise of each carrying on as they had been was reached and all three staff left the room feeling defeated.

Week 11

About three weeks before Christmas, Vicky developed a heavy cold and, after trying to struggle on for a day or two, was clearly too ill to continue and had to go off sick: it turned out to be flu and she was signed off work for at least a week. Jan, feeling very guilty, breathed a sigh of relief and found herself actually looking forward to going in to school the next day! She was not, however, prepared for the children's reactions. That evening she phoned Sara as she just had to talk over what had happened:

> JAN: *You won't believe what happened today. The children were so upset that they wouldn't be seeing 'Miss Vicky' for a few days that I had to help them make cards for her. Some of them were actually crying – I was just amazed. [The momentary silence at the other end of the phone told Jan that Sara was not so surprised.]*
>
> SARA: *I wish you two could see things from my perspective, Jan. You both put the children first and they know it – that's why they love her too.*

Week 12

One week later Vicky was still unable to return to work so the supply teacher remained. As she observed how this teacher dealt rather vaguely with the children's little disputes and worries, Jan began to realize that she and Vicky were very much in agreement over the fundamentals of good nursery practice.

Week 13

Vicky returned in the final week of term – still not well but determined to be there for the Christmas celebrations. She had been overwhelmed by the children's cards to her and knew that Jan must have given them a great deal of support, so when she thanked the children, she made a point of mentioning Jan in particular and noted Jan's pleased smile. The week passed in a hectic rush and once the children had finished, Vicky went straight home, too exhausted to go on the staff night out or to care what anyone thought of her!

Term 2

Week 1

It began with terrible weather, and no outdoor play was possible for the first few days. Four new children started nursery and were, as expected, tearful and demanding:

> VICKY: *Isn't it great to see how the children are helping these new little ones — they've come a long way since September, haven't they?*

> JAN: *I was just thinking about that. They're the best bunch I've had for a long time.*

> VICKY: *Well, we must be doing something right between us!* (Please let her agree with me!)

> JAN: *I reckon we are, Vicky.*

(Readers are invited here, before reading on further, to speculate on developing the scenarios leading to a 'happy ending'!)

By Easter Sara found that she was going into the nursery for light relief! She would be met with smiles and an invitation to come and see the latest display or hear about the plans for next week. It was very clear that the children were at ease and yet purposeful, turning expectantly to either Jan or Vicky when needing help or looking for praise.

●●● Analysis

Was it simply luck that Jan and Vicky resolved their differences? Sometimes such situations remain so difficult that one or other member of staff chooses to leave, despite both having the children's best interests at heart. Could it be that Sara's support for Jan or Vicky's readiness to learn influenced the outcome? Is it down to personalities or do school/nursery systems also play a part? Most important of all, what can we learn from this situation?

Let us first examine what led to the problems between these two characters. Their histories inform us that experience to date had probably caused them to form rather different views of what constitutes good early years practice. But both Jan and Vicky are clearly committed and caring practitioners, so how can this happen? It could suggest that one of the prime reasons is the difference in the initial training of nursery nurses and teachers.

Teacher training is a degree-level course, either through a three or four year degree or through a post-graduate certificate in education following completion of a relevant degree. Professional studies modules give students the skills of teaching and of meeting the children's developmental needs as part of the pedagogy, while curriculum studies concentrate on the National Curriculum subjects. At the same time students must follow their specialist subject such as maths, English, science, drama or early years.

Traditional nursery nurse (or childcare and education practitioner) training, provided by the Council for Awards in Child Care and Education (CACHE)/ Nursery Nurse Examination Board (NNEB), involves a two-year A-level equivalent course at college or school. There is a strong practical focus on caring skills as well as on providing educational activities, since the course qualifies students to work with babies and toddlers in full-day care settings, as well as with children aged from 3 to 8 years. CACHE students learn how children develop, how to provide nutritious meals and to offer appropriate rest and exercise to the youngest children, how to recognize illness and deal with first-aid emergencies. Much emphasis is placed on healthy social and emotional development and the need for practitioners to offer praise and reassurance, especially where these are lacking at home. They are made aware of child protection issues and of how to distinguish illness or failure to thrive from abuse. A major focus of the course is the value of play and the provision of an appropriate and stimulating environment in all early years settings. While cognitive and linguistic development is included, they are no more important then any other aspect of the course. Students must learn to cope with the relatively slow pace of the baby room in a day nursery and yet also be able to manage within the more structured regime of a Year 1 class in an infant school. A significant part of the course focuses on the needs of very young children and this fosters in the students powerful instincts of care and protection, which can make the adjustment to a school environment a difficult one.

When compared with initial teacher training it could be argued that there is more emphasis for nursery nurses on the nurturing aspect of early years work than is the case for teachers who, from the start of their course, must think about how to manage large numbers of young children in order to be able to teach them effectively. Of course there is a need for all early years practitioners to have warm and supportive relationships with the children in their care, but I would suggest that differences in emphasis in the roles of teachers and nursery nurses result in nursery nurses concerning themselves rather more with individual relationships with the children than with group dynamics. There are some advantages to such an approach, in terms of noticing developmental delay or spotting just why a child is having difficulty with a particular task: but it is also true that nursery nurses may have less experience of planning for and managing large groups of children.

Yet if the partnership is working well, each role will complement the other to create an effective team. Arguably what they were doing right was that Jan realized that she was trusting the children a little more since absorbing some of Vicky's philosophy that the children were capable of managing many tasks, such as clearing up after painting, with minimum support. Similarly Vicky recognized the value of Jan's nurturing approach and was now more at ease with offering constant reassurance to the less confident children.

●●● So why are there problems?

The relationship between the characters in the story illustrates some of the problems. The following summary outlines the issues and asks you to do some thinking.

Personality differences

This has to be expected in any working relationship, but especially where there is a hierarchy leading to an imbalance of power, such as is the case here.

What were your feelings upon being introduced to your first mentor in your school placement?

Training

As noted above, this informs the approach taken to most aspects of the education and care of young children.

How do you think it might make a difference to the way you communicate with 4 and 5-year-old children if you were to spend some time working with 2-year-olds?

Past experience

This may have been gained during training or subsequent employment. Practitioners often explain their beliefs about good practice in terms of observing a particular tactic, used by a more experienced colleague, which either worked well or failed disastrously. There is a powerful and sometimes unacknowledged element of the apprenticeship system at work here. Vicky's belief in the need for parent appointments is an example of this.

Can you recall an example from your own training when you observed a teacher use a technique which you decided to use yourself, or vowed to avoid at all costs? Have you done so?

Lack of trust in a colleague

Here Jan's earlier enthusiasm has been replaced by resentment, feeling unappreciated and ultimately making decisions with no reference to her colleague. As well as the negative impact on both practitioners, there is clearly a less pleasant, coherent and consistent environment for the children.

Lack of support from other staff/head/manager

In this case Sara managed her role with real tact, but possibly with too little concern for Vicky. The headteacher (Carol) tried to reassure Vicky but, in effect, applied more pressure by clearly expecting partnership in the Nursery without assisting the staff to achieve it.

You may wish to look again at the conversation Carol had with Vicky (pp 90–1) and write her a new script as if she had herself experienced a similar situation when first qualified.

Barriers to carrying out their role properly

Sometimes these are unintentional, such as lack of clear support for staff. They may also result from poor communication within a school or from an authoritarian management structure.

Were there any barriers in Treetops school? If so, why did they exist and how might they have been removed or reduced?

●●● Other key issues

Power-sharing can be difficult for nursery nurses who often have much experience but feel they are 'passed over', denied a voice in decisions, excluded from staff meetings or training days, and rarely invited to express an opinion to other professionals such as the health visitor. Some nursery nurses are happy to leave the responsibility to the teacher, but others are not, since they believe that their training has prepared them to do more than follow instructions. Yet when teachers do share responsibility for planning, they sometimes find that nursery nurses resent taking an equal part while they earn much less.

Recent work I have carried out with some newly qualified teachers identified further issues. One said of her initial difficulties with the nursery nurse that 'after four long years of training it was really hard to share my class with anyone else!' Another felt that she needed to take control quickly because the blame for any problems would ultimately lie with her; her nursery nurse was used to a more relaxed teacher and found this change very trying! Yet another had found almost the exact opposite in that she took over from a situation where the teacher and nursery nurse had worked successfully together for several years and felt she could not live up to expectations. Yet there were many positive comments as well. One teacher had found it very helpful to have an older, more experienced nursery nurse, who was sensitive and gave gentle hints when needed. Another said that, while the nursery nurse 'frightened the life out of me at first', she realized that here was someone who knew the ropes and could be depended upon and asked for help, which was gladly offered. Clearly sensitivity is required from both parties and, of course, there is no guarantee of this in any setting. But it is at least a useful starting point to be informed about the training of those with whom we work in order to better understand their approach.

For nursery nurses who have usually trained and perhaps worked in social services, private and voluntary organization nurseries, in private homes and in hospitals as well as in education, there can be the feeling that teachers have quite a restricted experience by comparison. Some believe that it is difficult to understand 5-year-olds if a practitioner has never worked closely with much younger children and find that there are teachers who tend not to respect their knowledge and contribution, apart from using them to carry out the more menial tasks of cleaning up vomit, changing children who have wet or soiled themselves and dealing with sick children! Some have reported to me that while they are considered capable of dealing with the difficult and disruptive child on a day-to-day basis, when the educational psychologist arrives they are not even consulted, let alone included in the formal meetings. As might be expected this could lead to frustration at being unable to voice their opinions, resentment and a feeling of inferiority.

We might ask ourselves if this attitude towards nursery nurses stems from teachers believing themselves to be on an equal footing with other professionals because they are trained to degree level, while nursery nurse training has only recently been recognized as the equivalent of A-levels (CACHE, 2003). There is currently a more general debate concerning the equivalence of practical, vocational training versus purely academic courses and one result of this has been the introduction of foundation degrees which recognize the skill and knowledge of experienced practitioners and enable them to gain the necessary qualification while remaining in work. Perhaps this will endorse the value of initial vocational training but, despite the facts of the matter, people's preconceived notions about each other's training can be a barrier to working in partnership. Hence I believe that there is a significant responsibility upon the training institutions to address this issue.

On the other hand, some nursery nurses report that working with a capable and confident teacher can be quite liberating, allowing them to use their real strengths of working with and supporting individual children and devising creative activities for small groups. They are content that the teacher is 'in charge' and do not wish to have responsibility for planning and documentation. For newly qualified teachers, it can therefore be quite difficult to gauge just what is expected of them by the nursery nurse particularly, in a nursery class setting.

●●● Creating and maintaining effective partnerships

Wilson and Charlton (1997: 10) suggest that a successful partnership will 'deliver more than the sum of its individual components' and, hence, benefit all involved. But Bastiani (1993: 104) contends that the term 'partnership' is used too readily, as if it were easy to achieve and commonplace. He considers it more useful to think in terms of 'working towards partnership', an important reminder of the need for ongoing review and effort. He draws upon the views of the early years writers Gillian Pugh, Sheila Wolfendale and Mary Drummond to produce the following list of what makes for a successful partnership (1993: 105):

● sharing of power, responsibility and ownership – though not necessarily equally

● a degree of mutuality, which begins with the process of listening and incorporates responsive dialogue and 'give and take'

● shared aims and goals, based on common ground, but which acknowledge important differences

● a commitment to joint action, in which parents, children and professionals work together.

This combination of principles and action seems particularly relevant today when new policies and practices are making constant demands on early years settings. What would it mean in practice in a nursery class setting to share power but 'not necessarily equally'? I would suggest further principles to the above list to achieve such power-sharing:

- *Respect based upon knowledge of each other's roles* – since this leads to understanding and removes mistaken assumptions (e.g. the belief that nursery nurses usually work only with babies and do not therefore understand the early years curriculum).

- *Clearly defined roles and responsibilities* – to enable each person to plan, consider and give of his or her best and to promote harmony (e.g. the teacher may have decided the theme for that half-term but could well ask the nursery nurse to choose the stories/creative activities for one particular week).

- *Good communication with clear times dedicated to open discussion* – when work is busy and the only communication tends to happen in snatched moments, there is often overlap of some duties which means that time is wasted and other jobs overlooked. Consider the difference to teamwork it would make to find time to sit down together to clarify roles and anticipate major difficulties in advance. For example, clear plans for that term's theme mean that resources are ordered and prepared in time, outings are organized, parents are informed and each person knows what is expected of him or her.

- *A sense of shared purpose which can help define problems and find solutions* – since most jobs have their difficult times or issues, working together can not only reduce the stress but can also lead to new and better arrangements. For example, consider a behaviour management issue, where the Nursery staff are trying a particular technique for a difficult child; the sense of working together can reduce the strain considerably and improve support for the child.

- *Willingness to reflect, evaluate and accept change* – many authors have stressed the need to respond to the observations we make of children, a central feature of early years practice, by constantly reviewing and adapting our practice (Abbott and Moylett, 1999; QCA, 2000; Sharman *et al.*, 2000; Miller *et al.*, 2002). For example, what would be the benefits *for partnership* of using the model Pugh (1998: 48) suggests, of the 'Practitioner's wheel' for the large construction area in the Nursery?

This consists of:

- planning
- implementing with suitable resources
- observing, supporting and extending
- observing and recording progress
- reflecting
- evaluating and adapting.

●●● Conclusions

This chapter has considered the individual players and some of the issues which may arise in a school setting. What of government and training issues?

While the current disparity in the salary and status of teachers and nursery nurses remains, it seems likely that a certain degree of unease between them will remain concerning their working relationship. Some early years centres, such as Pen Green, decided to put all early years staff on the same conditions since the available research indicated that differential terms of service 'appeared to be a real block to a creative partnership' (Whalley, 2001: 126). Whether other centres will follow suit remains to be seen, so what other possible ways are there of removing barriers to full partnership? Abbott and Moylett (1999: 180) consider the option of 'interprofessional training opportunities' to promote a more multi-disciplinary approach in early years settings. However they offer the valid criticism that rather than truly seeking to provide services appropriate for different age groups, this could simply be 'tinkering at the edges' of professional identities and interests while still remaining agency orientated. Yet it may well be that relationships which develop from such meetings start to remove divisive barriers, albeit on a small scale.

Inevitably the day-to-day reality of working well with colleagues depends to a large extent on the ethos of the individual school. For best practice, Lawrence believes that what is good for the children will also support the staff, claiming that 'The feeling of belonging to a worthwhile group could be the aim of the whole school approach to self-esteem enhancement' (1996: 45). This has been my experience, even when there have been difficulties instituting new work practices, or too few staff. There will always be different points of view about best practice in any setting and it's likely that there is rarely one absolutely right answer.

Roffey (2001: 1), an ardent promoter of co-operation and collaboration to achieve effectiveness, particularly when there are children with special needs, reminds us of the African proverb that 'It takes a village to raise a child'. This is not simply saying that there should be *many* people involved, but rather that there will be *different* people who will all contribute in their own way: an interesting and challenging thought as we allocate responsibility in our teams and communicate with parents. Perhaps in creating early years settings that demonstrate best practice, our most important aim should be to create a positive atmosphere where everyone, including the children and parents, has a voice and where ideas can be tried out in safety.

●●● References

Abbott, L. and Hevey, D. (2001) 'Training to work in the early years: developing the climbing frame', in G. Pugh (ed.) *Contemporary Issues in the Early Years.* London: Paul Chapman Publishing.

Abbott, L. and Moylett, H. (1999) *Early Education Transformed.* Lewes: Falmer Press.

Bastiani, J. (1993) 'Parents as partners', in P. Munn (ed.) *Parents and Schools.* London: Routledge.

Bruce, T. (1997) *Early Childhood Education.* London: Hodder & Stoughton.

CACHE (2003) *Diploma in Child Care and Education.* St. Albans, Hertfordshire: CACHE.

Lawrence, D. (1996) *Enhancing Self-esteem in the Classroom.* London: Paul Chapman Publishing.

Miller, L., Drury, R. and Campbell, R. (2002) *Exploring Early Years Education and Care.* London: David Fulton.

Pugh, G. (1998) *Quality in diversity in Early Learning – a Framework for Early Childhood Practitioners.* London: National Children's Bureau.

QCA (2000) *Curriculum Guidance for the Foundation Stage.* London: QCA.

Roffey, S. (2001) *Special Needs in the Early Years: Collaboration, Communication and Co-ordination.* London: David Fulton.

Sharman, C., Cross, W. and Vennis, D. (2000) *Observing Children.* London: Cassell.

Whalley, M. (2001) 'Working as a team', in G. Pugh (ed.) *Contemporary Issues in the Early Years.* London: Paul Chapman Publishing.

Wilson, A. and Charlton, K. (1997) *Making Partnerships Work.* York: York Publishing Services.

●●● Chapter 8

Making the most of an extra pair of hands: teachers and student teachers in the classroom

Deborah Smith and Deirdre Hewitt

Having student teachers in our classrooms is a frequent occurrence in today's climate of school-based training. A teacher may, over the course of one school year, be involved in the training of and working alongside a range of students undertaking a wide variety of academic and vocational qualifications. As well as student teachers, there are those studying for a variety of National Vocational Qualifications and school students undertaking work experience for the first time. Working alongside each requires skills, some of which are generic to working with all students, others that are particular to the course the student is undertaking. In our own teaching experience we have worked alongside many students, spanning 40 years as teachers in primary schools between us. It is this experience and, more recently, that of working within teacher training at a university college of higher education, that we draw upon for the main body of this chapter. Our experience is based upon working with student teachers at all levels of their course. We concentrate on these students and the development of skills required for their school block experience. The focus is on students studying for a teacher training qualification.

The chapter is in two main sections, one dealing with the issue of communication between teachers and students and the other with teachers' and student teachers' expectations of collaborative work. We intend to use these areas to examine our own practice and encourage other teachers to look critically at their own. We are by no means experts in the field of working with student teachers. However, we do have an enthusiasm for the process of collaborative work and a belief that the experience of working alongside students within our settings should be both rewarding and challenging for all concerned.

●●● Communication

Schools are 'hotbeds' of communication. Much of the English curriculum is concerned with enabling our children to become proficient communicators. However, do we, as teaching professionals, view this as something we should be both modelling and developing in our own dealings with student teachers? Some would argue that communication is a human need and an entitlement for all. Advertisements frequently proclaim 'It's good to talk!' Methods of communication abound in this digital age. Children are frequently very adept at communicating digitally yet lack the necessary skills to communicate successfully in person with another human adult. In this chapter we argue that, not only is it vital that we, as teachers, actively encourage children to communicate with one another successfully, but that we also extend this to include the student teachers within our classrooms to do the same. We discuss the reasons why this is important, looking specifically at how this knowledge will transfer into students' teaching. The practical implications are discussed and helpful hints suggested. Scenarios are described and questions for discussion raised. The hope is that these will highlight difficulties in communication between teachers and student teachers and affirm teachers' good practice in communicating with students.

Scenario 1: Elizabeth

The headteacher of your school has recently informed you that you are to have a second-year undergraduate teaching student, Elizabeth, assigned to your class for a five-week teaching block. 'Great!' you think. 'Finally the time to catch up on that non-contact time you were promised last September!' Monday arrives and so does Elizabeth, the aforementioned student. She informs you that she will be visiting one day a week for the next five weeks before starting her practice. For the remainder of these five visits she arrives at 8.45 am, five minutes before school starts. She completes all tasks you ask of her. However, she seems to have no real idea of the purpose of these visits. At the end of the day she leaves promptly at 3.45 pm before any of the school's permanent staff.

The above scenario presents the teacher with some problems. The student teacher's attendance is good, as is her punctuality. However, there seems to be a lack of commitment and lack of understanding that the role of teacher extends beyond the contact hours with the children. The class teacher may be worried that this timekeeping may continue when the practice starts and may prevent adequate communication about planning and preparation taking place. How can this be addressed prior to the block practices being started?

This scenario highlights many issues which could have been avoided with improved communication between participants. The class teacher appears to have received little information about the student from the headteacher. She needs information regarding the purpose of these attachment days, at the very least. The responsibility for this rests with Elizabeth, as she will have been given details from her college tutors. However, a common occurrence is that a copy of the handbook for student placements had been sent to the school but remained within the headteacher's office. If the class teacher had a copy she could both direct and encourage Elizabeth to complete relevant tasks that would then feed into her block practice.

The class teacher is also worried by Elizabeth's timekeeping. The school probably has an agreed start and minimum finish time for all teachers. Many schools do have this and details about start and finish times are probably to be found within the staff handbook. However, for whatever reasons, this has not been communicated to Elizabeth and the class teacher is unsure of whether this applies to students. The time Elizabeth spends in school may be seen as a reflection of her commitment to the task in hand. Few teachers, if any, arrive five minutes before the children do and leave promptly at the end of the day. There is much to do outside contact hours with the children, yet Elizabeth seems to have little understanding of this fact.

We would suggest that improved communication between teachers and student teachers from the very first visit would mean such situations would be less likely to occur. A very effective method, which also saves time, is to have a student handbook presented to all students on their first visit. An eager student can bombard the teacher with questions regarding the school day and appropriate timekeeping. This information can be included within the handbook to enable the student to become quickly familiar with routines and refrain from asking unnecessary questions of already very busy teachers. The handbook can contain facts about the school that the student needs to know and could also ask questions about the student that the school would like answered in order for attachment and block practice to be most effective.

Questions could include the following:

● What experience of teaching have you already undertaken?
● What are the tasks to be carried out on attachment days, as set by college?

- What areas do you see as your strengths?
- What areas would you like support in to enable you to develop more fully?

This would enable even the most reticent student teacher to communicate his or her thoughts to the class teacher or school-based mentor. Many students simply do not want either to bother the teacher with too many questions or requests or do not know which information they need either to seek from or to offer to the school.

Why do teachers need to communicate with students?

- In order to know what each other is doing (teaching progress).
- So that the student can learn how to do things (teaching methods).
- To know what practice is expected to occur (teaching expectations).
- To give feedback and advice on teaching (mentoring student teaching).

The above reasons indicate that effective communication is a vital part of the mentoring process. When working with students it is important to use a variety of communication techniques in appropriate ways. There are those methods of communication that we view as formal, such as written recording of observations and discussions and those that are more informal, such as daily discussions on what has been achieved during that day. Much of the role of the professional teacher is that of mentor, working alongside, coaching and advising students within a classroom situation. It is here that students can put the theory learned in college into practice. This is often the part students say they most enjoy.

It is our belief that this process of mentoring works best when the mentor and class teacher is the same person. The class teacher mentor has daily contact with the student whereas a more 'remote' mentor may only meet with the student once per week for a formal observation and feedback. It can be argued that a more 'remote' mentor may be in a better position to give an objective opinion because he or she has not invested so much time and energy in supporting the student (see Campbell and Kane, 1996, for further discussion of being too close to a student teacher). So much informal communication goes on daily between the class teacher and student that it is in fact invaluable to the mentoring process. The class teacher observes so much more than one lesson per week. One teacher we observed took the role of classroom assistant supporting the student for the duration of her teaching. This enabled her to take an active part in the class throughout the student's teaching experience block placement. The class teacher is also the person who knows the children best and so is most appropriately suited to guiding the student to set challenging yet achievable targets and objectives for the children as a whole class and as individuals. The following case study portrays how effective the role of the class teacher could be in helping a student achieve her potential in teaching practice during her school block placement.

Scenario 2: Pamela

Pamela was a fourth year student assigned to a Year 2 class within an inner-city primary school. The class teacher, Mrs Jones, was a very experienced Key Stage 1 practitioner. The mentor within the school was Mrs Turner, the deputy head-teacher, who taught full time within the Foundation Stage unit within the school. Mrs Turner carried out weekly formal observations of Pamela teaching and gave formal feedback when targets for the forthcoming week were agreed and recorded. Other than that weekly contact, they only saw each other on the odd occasion when they happened to be within the staffroom at the same time, which was not often, due to Mrs Turner's management duties.

However, the class teacher, Mrs Jones, had regular daily discussions and communications with Pamela throughout her practice. She had advised Pamela on possible teaching activities at the planning stage, although it was the mentor, Mrs Turner, who had formally agreed these plans. Each morning Mrs Jones and Pamela met to discuss the day's activities. This gave Mrs Jones the chance to provide helpful hints that could aid Pamela's teaching. At the end of each day they discussed how the lessons went. Pamela frequently, at the very beginning of the practice, used these times to discuss children's progress or lack of it with Mrs Jones. This was invaluable in helping her plan to meet each child's learning needs. During such conversations Pamela was quite candid in discussing her own teaching and how she could evaluate and improve it.

The above scenario demonstrated how effective the class teacher could be through methods of informal communication. These conversations between teacher and student can help both achieve their aims. The student was able to ask questions about children's achievement and her own teaching in a non-threatening situation. The teacher was able to guide the student about the children's abilities as she answered her questions. She could provide support and encouragement on a daily basis. Engaging in this informal communication exchange can help the student develop her understanding of how children learn and what is the most appropriate method of meeting their needs. Not all students and teachers establish such a trusting relationship in which both can communicate freely. Some practitioners are very effective communicators with the children within their class yet tend to remain reticent with students who are working in their class. They may not, for whatever reason, feel confident about their role as mentor. They may not have received formal training in the role and so feel they do not know what the role entails. They could perhaps feel threatened by the presence of a student within their class. However, if these issues are not addressed, they will affect the quality of communication between themselves and the student. First and foremost the student is within their class to learn. He or she has been assigned to that class because the management within the school believes the teacher is both competent and experienced. This experience enables the teacher to guide the student through his or her block practice.

From the very first visit it is useful for the teacher to talk to the student about what he or she expects from his or her practice. If informal methods of communication are not established early on then there could be an over-reliance on formal methods. Discussions to evaluate the progress the student is making will be need to be made more regularly than the usual once per week teaching observation and feedback. As previously mentioned, we believe that the informal conversations that take place between experienced practitioners and students are vital to the student achieving his or her potential with regards to teaching ability.

Modelling teaching can be a very useful tool for the teacher who has tried to talk to the student about an area of his or her teaching that needs further development. This type of advice through modelling is not always taken up by the student. This can be frustrating for the teacher. Modelling a lesson and demonstrating the advice within a practical setting can help support the teacher's previous observations and comments. A student might also request that the teacher model a particular technique so that he or she can see what the practice actually entails. An example of how modelling can work can be illustrated by the story of a student who admitted to one of us that she was unsure and lacking in confidence about how to teach physical education with a Reception class. One of us, a classroom teacher at the time, agreed to teach a demonstration PE lesson. The student completed a formal observation schedule during this lesson. She was able to identify strengths and possible improvements from being in the role of observer. Following on from the lesson, the teacher and student discussed the lesson in detail picking out techniques for behaviour management with which the student had lacked confidence.

●●● Teachers' and student teachers' expectations of collaboration

In reflecting on the word 'expectation' it is interesting to study the synonyms given in *Collins Gem 'Thesaurus'*: 'anticipation, confidence, expectancy, foresight, hope, prospect, reliance, trust.'

In this section of the chapter we hope to show just how relevant these meanings are when dealing with teacher/student expectations. What exactly are the teacher's expectations when a student is to arrive on the scene? Are they about the amount of non-contact and preparation time that is to be anticipated, or is it the challenge, prospects and enthusiasm that a student teacher will bring to the school?

To be a mentor is to be in an extremely privileged position. We can remember the familiar scenario of the young child who believes that everything the teacher says is the absolute gospel truth. Most of us have experienced the following conversation between a child and her parent: 'No, Mum, I cannot wear blue ribbons, my teacher said', or 'That is not the way to do multiplication, my teacher showed me how.' Teacher definitely knows best! To a large extent this is the same for the trainee and the mentor. It is particularly so for a student early on in his or her training. He or she has the chance to meet 'a real live teacher'! The possible influence the teacher can have is incredible. It is the teacher to whom the student will look for a role model, and to show the standard expected by the teaching profession.

In university the conversation is often mirrored with tutors and students: 'Well, that is not the way my teacher did it!' or 'My teacher said this is the most effective method.' And we all know, at the end of the day, teacher knows best! The school-based placement is the opportunity to bridge the gap between the university training and the reality of the classroom and an opportunity to fuse theory and practice. Janet Colvert, East Sussex County Schools' Adviser (cited in Holmes, 1999), believes that, in order to bridge the gap successfully, 'there must be a real partnership where the Mentor and trainee are both committed to the ongoing educational debate that marks the reflective practitioner'. It is the student teacher's chance to put into practice what he or she has previously only heard or read about. Understandably they arrive in the classroom with mixed emotions. As with most other relationships it is through talking to someone that you understand them better. It has been said that teachers should keep close to their hearts a corked bottle containing their childhood and, I would add, their student memories too. Uncorking the bottle when appropriate would release empathy and enhance understanding. Teachers should be reminded to uncork their bottles and think back to those early days in front of a class!

What are the practical implications of such an insight? Janet Colvert has used the word 'partnership'. I would like to take this concept a step further. Let's look carefully at what a true partnership entails. It actually incorporates some of the qualities used to define 'expectation'. To have a true partnership there must be honesty, openness, trust, confidence and reliance. All these qualities must be grouped under the umbrella of 'professionalism'. As with all partnerships and relationships in schools, there must be a professional dimension. There will be times, as in any partnership, when honesty will be required, even when the truth may cause hurt and uncomfortable feelings. But as with all situations in life, 'It's not what you say, it's the way that you say it'! Yet the truth is vital; arguably even more for the female gender which dominates the teaching profession. Think of a scenario involving shopping where a good 'shopping partner' is asked: 'Does my bottom look big in this?' If it does then you would hope the trusted person would say 'Yes!' One useful rule of thumb in personal and professional life: treat others as you would wish to be treated yourself.

This is exemplified in the following discussion about a lesson observation. Instead of telling the student what he or she has done wrong, you could ask him or her the following questions:

- What did you think of the lesson?
- What went well in the lesson?
- What would you not do again?
- How could it be improved?
- What did the children learn?
- How do you know what the children learned – what evidence do you have?

Hopefully, the student will have already identified the areas for development. In our experience student teachers are frequently very harsh on themselves, but it is sometimes much easier to develop and build on their criticism than to initiate the criticism yourself. The student will then expect some constructive advice from the teacher, so he or she can learn from his or her mistakes. Without reflection there will be little or no learning. It is through discussion that real long-term learning is assured, not forgetting that the definition of discussion is that both parties 'listen' to each other. From our experience of mentoring, we have found that adults tend to take errors personally and are more likely to let criticism affect their self-esteem. This may lead to a tendency to apply tried and tested methods, thus taking fewer risks. One way to encourage them to try new methods is to model them.

We would advocate the Vygotskian method of learning. Vygotsky believed that adults should treat the student as an apprentice. The process can be likened to an apprentice in industry. The apprentice is shown in great detail how to develop skills. This process is slow and intensive, thus allowing the apprentice to master the intricacy of the profession, repetition being the key. The apprentice begins with simple tasks, building up to amalgamating the simpler task into an intricate product. In educational speak, the apprentice experiences the 'zone of proximal development'. In this zone each day leads to a higher level of ability. Usually the zone of proximal development refers to the instructional stage in learning, where the potential ability of a child can be recognized. The process takes learners, with adult support, just beyond their present achievements in a sort of 'scaffolding' of student learning by the teacher. We would strongly argue that this applies to adult learning, too! The zone of proximal development, we would suggest, is also the site of the maturation of the student teachers' ideas. These ideas have been planted, germinated and sown by university tutors and teachers. However, it is in the capable hands of the dedicated mentor that the flower buds will surely open.

Bruner saw adult assistance as vital. In his explanation of 'how the more competent assist the young and less competent to reach that higher ground from which to reflect more abstractly about the nature of things' he demonstrates the value of assistance (1986: 73). Obviously the student is less competent, less experienced than the teacher, but it is through careful, sensitive negotiation that students are nurtured and can develop and grow into professional, efficient teachers. However, we believe there is also a problem with this. Unless you are very clear about what you are seeing when you observe, good practice can appear effortless and seamless, and it may be difficult to identify what there is to learn. Discussion should both precede and follow an observation in order to maximize the learning opportunities.

Scenario 3: A PGCE student observes your literacy lesson although this is in a different key stage from the class in which she is doing her practice

The teacher, Miss Smith, is talking through her planning. She is involving the student in the actual planning of the lesson. In this way the student can appreciate where the lesson fits in with the medium-term planning. A dialogue follows where the student can ask questions of the teacher, thus ascertaining why certain activities have been chosen. Following the planning stage, the student is then more equipped to anticipate how the lesson will unfold and to understand the direction that the lesson is taking. The classroom teacher also gave 'asides' during the lesson, taking the time to explain why she had just guided the lesson along a particular course or why she had used a pupil's question in a certain way. The student found this to be very effective. The discussion that followed between the teacher and the student was much more informed and in-depth.

It is through involving the student in the planning, delivery and evaluation that expectations are carefully communicated. The high standards of teaching and learning set within the school, among staff and within the classroom, are clearly communicated to the student, without having to be dictatorial or domineering. Presumably the student has freely chosen to enter the teaching profession and therefore wishes to become a competent, effective teacher, embracing the expectations both explicitly and implicitly. As the quotation below demonstrates, there is a need for problem-solving in an individualized way to enhance students' learning: 'We must recognise that adults want their learning to be problem-orientated, personalised and accepting of their need for self-direction and personal responsibility' (www.coe.sdsu.edu/eet/Articles/index.htm).

As can be seen from the discussion of the role of the mentor, the mentor performs many roles:

- *Supporter* –allowing the students to believe in themselves, developing their confidence and self-esteem.
- *Discriminating, critical friend* – knowing when and how much to intervene, offering appropriate guidance.
- *Appraiser and judge* – demonstrating thought and sensitivity.

- *Planner and reflective practitioner* – knowing at what point the student can work independently and helping critical reflection.
- *Challenger* – remembering to make the challenge realistic and achievable.
- *Coach and peer counsellor* – modelling effective practice.

To work collaboratively with the trainee models good practice, implicitly communicating the value of working with colleagues. Just as the merit of children working collaboratively in pairs or groups is widely recognized so, too, should be the merit of conversing openly with the student: 'There is now an extensive body of evidence, which shows that getting children to work collaboratively in pairs or small groups can help them to develop their skills in conceptual understanding' (Wood and O'Malley, 1996). Arguably this applies as much to student teachers as to children. To take this one step further, if a student observes a particularly effective technique being used, but is not given the opportunity to reflect with the teacher, to question and further promote understanding, a vital learning opportunity is missed. Unfortunately not all students are eager to work collaboratively with the teacher, or vice versa. Problems can then arise.

Scenario 4: Gill, a mature student on her second school experience

Gill comes on a weekly basis to observe, before starting her five-week school experience placement. She soon realizes that the children in the Year 2 class are quite demanding, many of the children having special educational needs and a high proportion of children with social problems. Gill also realizes that one particular child, Billy, is particularly challenging! The class teacher carefully and in detail explains Billy's home life, which is certainly not experienced by the average child. She explains his history since entering school in the nursery. Although there has been a degree of improvement, the staff still have grave concerns about his behaviour.

Time progresses in the placement and Gill reaches the second week. During this second week she rather naïvely confides in one of the staff colleagues that she does not think that the teacher's behaviour management is very effective. 'She simply does not shout enough!' Gill appears naïve because, as any experienced professional knows, you do not criticize one member of staff to another. Unbeknown to Gill, the class teacher is informed of her opinion! She choses to say nothing, but to allow Gill to handle the class in the way she knows best! Sure enough her voice is heard bellowing throughout Key Stage 1. Sure enough, she slowly but surely looses the control and respect of the class. The class teacher, after giving Gill ample opportunity to discuss the situation, finds that Gill finally realizes that she had tackled the situation unprofessionally and unproductively! Nevertheless, it was a path she had to take, she had to experience it for herself. She is now more open to the use of assertive discipline and she has accepted that, although the children's behaviour, particularly Billy's, is not perfect, it is probably the best that can be achieved in the circumstances. Perhaps Gill went on to use assertive discipline at home too, because we all know that often what we learn in the classroom, and from our children, affects how we treat others.

Kyriacou (1991: 92) comments: 'Dealing with pupil misbehaviour is not simply a matter of discipline, but is also bound up with your pastoral care responsibilities.' Kyriacou goes on to discuss the importance of mutual respect. This does not often happen quickly but, rather, it requires patience and time. The relationship took time to develop. Hopefully, at the end, the teacher was able to be a facilitator for Gill's learning.

We hope that, from reading this chapter, it has become apparent that the same principles of working with pupils in the class apply when working with trainee teachers. A good mentor will have the ability to motivate, challenge, give appropriate feedback and guidance, reflect and, most of all, allow the bud to open and begin its journey into a beautiful, colourful, sweet-smelling flower. Your expectations as a mentor should be high as you are leading a student on the long and winding road to teaching: leading him or her into one of the most rewarding, demanding and stimulating jobs one could possibly be gifted enough to encounter.

●●● References

Bruner, J. (1986) *Actual Minds, Possible Worlds*. Cambridge: Cambridge University Press.
Campbell, A. and Kane, I. (1996) 'Mentoring and primary school culture', in
   D. McIntyre, and H. Hagger (eds) *Mentoring in Schools: Developing the Profession of Teaching*. London: David Fulton.
Holmes, E. (1999) 'High hopes for a safe landing', *The Times Educational Supplement*, 7 May.
Kyriacou, C. (1991) *Essential Teaching Skills*. Oxford: Blackwell.
Wood, D. and O'Malley, C. (1996) 'Collaborative learning between peers: an overview', *Educational Psychology in Practice*, 11: 4–9.

●●● Chapter 9

All different, all equal: a case study of support at Temple Primary School

Anne Campbell

●●● Context

This chapter is based on individual and group interviews with adults and children from Temple Primary School in north Manchester. I am currently a governor at the school and I am a member of the curriculum, personnel and finance subcommittees. I regularly spend time in the school talking to staff, parents and children. I would like to thank all those who shared their views with me and who collaborated in this small project. After the views of the children will come those of the adults. The intention is to explore how teachers, support workers and children work together for the benefit of improving learning and making school a good place in which to be either an adult or a child.

The school has many interesting features. It is one of the first primary schools in the Private Finance Initiative (PFI) rebuilding programme and gained Pathfinder status, meaning it had a leading role in the development of PFI schools. The school moved into its new building in September 2001, from a very run-down, old and inadequate one. The 500 or so children attending Temple Primary School come from a wealth of different cultural backgrounds: 98 per cent speak English as an additional language. The pupils have predominantly Punjabi, Urdu, Arabic and Malay as their home language. In addition, pupils also speak another 11 languages.

There are 54 staff in the school consisting of teachers, assistant headteacher, deputy headteacher, headteacher, teaching assistants, learning mentors, nursery nurses, bilingual support teachers and instructors, lunchtime organizers, and administrative and clerical staff, but excluding catering and caretaking and cleaning staff who are employed and managed by the Facilties Management

Group under PFI rules. Staff members are either called teaching staff or associate staff depending on their role. There is a good ethnic mix within the staff and governors, nearly half of whom are from minority ethnic backgrounds. In addition to these staff, student teachers and other childcare students regularly undertake practice placements in the school. Parents are warmly welcomed as partners and support workers in the classrooms. Temple is a busy, vibrant, multicultural, inner-city primary school that has many challenges as well as many opportunities. The local area provides one of the main challenges, due to high levels deprivation, a high level of crime and poor levels of mental health. However, Ofsted (Report 252932) found the school to be a very good one, meeting the challenges presented by children and local area well, and found that:

> while test results are well below the national averages, pupils make good progress in response to effective teaching and very good learning experiences. Given their low attainment on entry, with many having limited skills in understanding and speaking English, pupils do particularly well to achieve the standards that they do. Excellent leadership and management provide a clear and successful focus for raising standards and improving provision. Pupils enjoy school, behave well and forge very good relationships. This is a very caring school where pupils are valued as individuals (2003: 1).

Like many other staff of similar schools, Temple staff members exhibit a high level of commitment to the pupils and strive very hard to make the children's time at school a happy, productive and enjoyable experience. All staff members are very serious about their children's welfare and work hard to provide the best learning environment they can.

●●● Out of the mouths of babes…

I wanted to give the children the opportunity to voice their opinions and allow them to give their perspectives on the support they receive from the many people who work in their school. I met two small groups of children of varying ages from 6 to 11, and explained that I wanted to talk to them about all those people who helped them in school for a book I was writing. I asked them the following questions:

- How long have you been at this school?
- Which adults work in the school?

- What jobs do they do?
- Which adults work in your classroom?
- What jobs do they do?
- How are they different from each other?
- How do they help you?

The children I talked to warmed easily to the topic, liking to talk about their classrooms and those who worked there. Apart from their innate inquisitive nature, the children at Temple are encouraged to find out about the working of the school and to participate in establishing a shared ethos and ways of working in their classrooms and school. There is a successful School Council, and the school motto, 'All different, all equal', indicates the approach to working within a diverse cultural and social context.

I illustrate the children's views through two 'fictional' children, one a young child of infant age whom I call Kamila, and one an older child in the last year of primary school, Munir. I hope to represent the differing perspectives by amalgamating the views of the children in the groups. This is a technique developed by Campbell and Kane (1998) in a book about school-based teacher education, which is located in a fictional primary school with fictional teacher, tutor and pupil characters but drawing on actual events and conversations. Similar to this small project the stories or fictions are based on empirical data collected through interview and diary notes. In another book, Cooper and Hyland (2000) collected stories from children about their lives at school, including stories about the adults who worked with them in their classrooms and schools, in particular about the student teachers who were placed on school-based experience. Hyland (in Cooper and Hyland, 2000: 22) justifies the use of pupil perceptions as follows:

> *Children's judgements are often acute, but some things may be too far beyond their present experience and maturity to appreciate. It seems to me that the ethical position is that pupils have a right to have their observations and opinions taken seriously, though I am not suggesting that we rely on them as the final judgement on the teaching they receive.*

It has become politically fashionable to ask children for their views on their teachers and their teaching, as proposed by the recent Ofsted framework for inspection of schools. It is not for that reason that I took the approach in this chapter. I wanted to gain a different perspective of support workers, and let the children tell the story from their point of view. After all, they spend a lot of time at the receiving end of teaching assistants and support workers.

The children I spoke to had varied backgrounds and differing lengths of time in school (e.g. one was the child of an asylum seeker who had been at the school for less than a year but whose English was impressive for such a short time). Another had been at the school since the Nursery class through to Year 6. The vast majority of the children interviewed spoke English as an additional language, this being a fair representation of the school population. All children were articulate and interested in the topic for discussion. The following views expressed by the two 'fictional' children are based on the discussions with the two small groups which I informally interviewed.

Kamila's perceptions

Kamila is in a Year 1 class and is 6 years old. She says she likes to come to school and she says she does lots of interesting things in her classroom. She was keen to talk to me and was very positive about all the adults she encountered: 'The people who work in my school are teachers, cooks, dinner ladies and cleaners.' There was no mention of teaching support staff. When asked about whether all the adults in her classroom are teachers, Kamila showed no hesitation in replying:

> Yes they are and all the teachers talk to you and they sort it out when there is an 'accident'. And they correct your work and tick it. Teachers are really nice to you. I really liked my teacher last year best because she did an assembly about friends and she called me out to the front because I was one of her friends. I like all of the teachers. We do lots of good things with our teachers, like drawing, writing and playing. The teachers help me to write better and to learn things. Miss W [teaching assistant] always helps us to tidy up at the end of the day. Miss R [teacher] does the register in the morning and does maths with us in our special books and always reads us a story at the end of the day. When my mum and dad come to school they talk to all of the teachers and ask about how I am getting on with my work.

Sometimes some teachers work with little groups of children if they have problems and need more help with their reading and writing. Sometimes I go in these groups with Miss W and I like it and we get to talk to her and ask her things. In the playground I hold Miss W's hand. The teachers help me to learn English. Some of them speak my language and help me understand things more.

And just in case the interviewer felt left out, a remark aimed at me: 'I like visitors that come to school too!'

Munir's perceptions

Munir has been at the school for most of his educational career and is now in the final class in Year 6. He is 11 years old and is very knowledgeable about the school. He says he enjoys his life at school:

> Adults do lots of jobs in school, like helping children, teaching and helping children who are getting bullied. They sometimes sit down and talk to you. There's a special place where you can go to talk about your problems with Miss X or Mr J. They are learning mentors who help you if you are having problems with bullying or someone does not like you. They help you sort out problems. They also give out merits and stickers and stars when you are good.

> Some of the adults are helpers, not teachers, who help you. Some are learning mentors and some are teachers and they don't have their own classes but they do the booster classes, like Miss D and some do Gifted and Talented like Ms S.

> The teachers organize clubs and groups like Yoga, Choir, Dance and Homework club for those who can't do their homework at home. The clubs are at lunchtime and at Friday after school. We also do Multi Sports and Computer and Library clubs.

> Sometimes the children are helpers too. They monitor the doors, the computers, do the milk and ring the bell. We also have the 'Friendship Squad' in the playground. The Friendship Squad are children who help those who have no one to play with in the playground. They wear red hats so you can tell who they are in the playground.

> I do know the meaning of learning mentor. They like to help in different ways. They help you learn about people and they teach you sometimes things like how to ride a bike properly and help with other projects. The learning mentor takes out children that have behaviour problems to help them learn how to behave better. I'm a 'learning mentor child' but my problem isn't behaviour. I have a problem with making friends. My learning mentor helps me make friends in the class and in the playground because most of the friends I make move off to Malaysia and Saudi Arabia

because their parents have come here to do tests like PhDs and degrees and stuff. My learning mentor will look out for me and help me make friends so that when I go to high school next year I won't be lonely and I'll have some friends from this school.

In our learning mentor books we get targets at the back and the learning mentor will write down when we do well and we'll get stickers when you meet them [the targets]. I was the first person to get 40 stickers! When you get 40 stickers you get a prize. One of the learning mentors is famous. If you go in the office you can see a picture of a learning mentor shaking David Beckham's hand. She won Football Coach of the Year and got to meet David Beckham at Old Trafford.

Teachers are different from learning mentors. They show you how to do work in literacy, maths, science, religious education and 'subjects'. Teachers also do SATs. I don't like SATs, only the maths ones. I don't like the other literacy SATs much.

●●● Discussion

One potential problem for children who did not have a learning mentor is that they may not have access to stickers! Life could be rather boring without stickers. Learning mentors mainly focus on supporting positive behaviour and on helping children get ready for learning through developing positive attitudes, raising self-esteem and levels of confidence. Therefore stickers and other symbolic recognitions of achievement are important.

Munir was quite clear about the differences between learning mentors and teachers, recognizing the difference between pastoral support and teaching subjects, although he was not aware that some teaching assistants and learning mentors ran after-school clubs as well as teachers. He clearly saw the difference between teachers teaching 'subjects' and learning mentors 'supporting' behaviour and the development of positive attitudes towards work and pupil–pupil relationships. He was aware of the 'targeted children' approach employed by the learning mentor support team, whereby certain children are identified as vulnerable and targeted for specific learning mentor support. He also understood that some teachers had 'specialist' roles (e.g. taking booster literacy groups or support groups for gifted and talented children). He knew the difference between class teachers and support teachers.

Younger children, such as Kamila, were not aware of any differences between learning mentors, teaching assistants and teachers. Kamila did know there was a difference between lunchtime organizers, cooks and caretakers: 'They don't work in the classroom and have very different jobs and wear a uniform.' The wearing of distinctively different clothes allied to their jobs (e.g. cook or kitchen staff) helped younger children identify people with different jobs. However, Kamila viewed all staff in the classroom and playground, regardless of their status, as teachers.

Older children, like Munir, were very clear about who did what and knew the proper terminology with regards to the different roles of adults. This was often reflected by personal experience. For instance, Munir was extremely knowledgeable about the welfare assistant, probably because his family had been involved in a situation where there had been a great deal of contact with the education welfare service. He was able to describe the role of the welfare assistant: 'She helps children get new clothes when they need them and gets them a social worker to help their parents too.'

Taking the time to explain what roles the different people in school have to the children would appear to reduce any stigma attached to different roles and increase the children's understanding of how school can help them and support their learning, socialization, friendships and experience of school life. Arguably the children at Temple, from my knowledge of the school and its inhabitants, are well placed to develop empathy with their peers and teachers. One instance of this is the Friendship Squad described earlier. Membership of the 'Friendship Squad' is highly sought after and children feel proud to have been chosen as part of this team. In the busy life of a modern primary school, employing a wide range of teachers and support workers, children can some-times be quite bewildered as to who does what unless time is taken to involve them in the organization and planning of the teaching and support for learn-ing. Children understanding that their classmates have differing needs and that a variety of people can provide different types of support would seem to help promote a good learning environment. There is a real sense of a learning com-munity where all participants are valued for their different kinds of support. Munir also acknowledges the contribution that children in the school make to the learning community. He recognizes that children teach and support each other and that they can learn from each other.

●●● Adults talking about their own and others' roles

I also talked individually with a number of staff from the school: teachers, learning mentors, parent helpers in the Nursery, bilingual instructors, teaching assistants and lunchtime organizers. In the same way as I have amalgamated perspectives and views from the children, several of the support workers' and teachers' views have been combined to illustrate the different roles of support workers and teachers. I approached these informal interviews with a loose structure in mind, asking the adults to talk to me about the following:

- What role do you have in the school?
- Can you tell me about your previous employment history?
- What successes, challenges, dilemmas or concerns can you tell about your job?
- How is your role organized and managed in the school?
- How is your work recognized and valued?
- What support and training is there for your role?

Bilingual support worker

I am a bilingual instructor and I work with several classes during the week. I belong to the Ethnic Minority Achievement Service [EMAS] and there is a co-ordinator in school who manages the work of the EMAS staff in school. We provide support and training services for children and staff. We help provide differentiated work for children whose first language is not English. We work collaboratively with the other staff in classrooms. We also do community-based work with parents and local people to help make better links with the school and improve communication in a number of languages.

Having more money for resources and staffing, and having more space would significantly improve my job and the jobs of other EMAS staff in the school. Also having more time to share good practice and swap ideas would improve our practice.

I do feel that the work I do is recognized and valued and that there is a professional approach to the management of staff. That has improved. The new Workload Agreement is not really making much of a difference as yet to the roles that we have. The management system we have in school does work well. People feel valued and listened to regardless of the job role you have.

The children are appreciative of the work that all adults do with them. There's something about the ethos in the school that promotes appreciation and value of all the community. We do have some difficulties in getting parents involved. We have to give them the confidence to work with children and other adults. For many parents that would mean providing language classes to learn English. I think the school motto – All different, All equal – says it all. It's a celebration of the differences in languages, cultures and backgrounds.

The parent support worker

I have a long association with school. I have six children and four of them have been through this school. I am now coming in to support in the classroom due to interest I now have in special educational needs. I have a child with special educational needs and I want to find out how to support that child and others in the same situation.

I'm not very clear about the different roles of teachers and support workers though I do accept the 'authority' of the teacher. Things have changed a lot since I was at school.

I would like to see more drama in the school. We need more support workers who can help in these Foundation subjects. There is too narrow a curriculum. I know which staff are interested in which subjects and can pull better work out from the children. I am interested in arts. I like to take the children to the art gallery. It's more indirect learning, rather than direct teaching. We need more child-friendly places for a wider education.

There are a lot of students who come in and support the teachers and some parents like me. I think we often take the staff for granted. There are 54 members of staff in this school and some parents just bring their children to school and leave them without realizing that there is a big team working here. The team has lots of different types of workers although I think parents just perceive learning mentors as teachers, particularly Miss X. They see her as the sports teacher. My child talks about his learning mentor and what he's been doing with her.

I sometimes don't know who is the support teacher or real teacher in some classes. I always think they do equal jobs. In some classes the teacher 'takes over' the class or is 'in control'. The teaching assistant supports and the teacher leads. As the children get older the differences are more noticeable between the roles of the different adults in the classroom.

When I am supporting children in class, it helps to have had experience of supporting my own children. I would like to see more parents, like me, in the classroom. It not only helps other children, it helps your own because you know more about what goes on in school and can help them more. The school is very welcoming and appreciates the work I do.'

The lunchtime organizer

As a lunchtime organizer I've done a bit of everything. I worked for a long time in the old school and now I'm in the new school. The best thing about my role is helping children adapt to school, making sure they settle in happily and helping children with behaviour problems. I try to understand what happens to them by watching over them. I also understand more because I have a child with behaviour problems myself.

Difficult and challenging children make me feel that I need more training for the job. I need more training on how to manage children's behaviour and how to control playground behaviour and make better connections with what goes on in class. We need better liaison with teachers and better strategies for games outside and some more training on child protection issues. I have had some training on these but feel I need more. I like working here and feel valued.

The learning mentor

I see my role as boosting attainment and self-esteem. I love to see the children growing in confidence. I work in class with a target group throughout the year. I monitor attendance and punctuality, phone parents up and visit if absence continues. If there are any problems anywhere I would tackle them, not just with my target group. It's a strange life being a learning mentor. I'm not a teacher and the children know I'm not a teacher. It's a fine line to walk, sometimes a dangerous line to walk. I have to be careful all the time. I've got to be there for the children to talk to. It's difficult if a child is in tears or upset due to something happening at school. I sometimes think the children think I am a child and they speak to me sometimes as if I was one of them. I do my best to help them but also have to tell them that if it is anything serious I have to tell the teacher or the head. Relationships with the teachers are very important. You can work with a teacher who you don't like or disagree with but you have to show the children that you can work professionally with other adults in school.

We are all very different learning mentors and we all take different approaches and do our own thing, We all do get on as people but mostly do what we are best at. At our team meetings we discuss what our roles are and what we are doing and any new initiatives, such as the walking bus that Miss X is doing (that's a scheme to pick up and walk with children on their way to school to help them be punctual and ensure they are safe on the way here). We also do Breakfast Club that makes sure children get a good breakfast and then there's Homework Club to help them finish their homework. It's sort of all-round care before, during and after school. Another challenge is working with older children who have very little English. I am doing a course about that at the moment. Unfortunately most of the courses for learning mentors are after school. I'd like to see us doing more daytime courses especially in behaviour management but there are funding issues and cover for the team if someone is out of school. Other learning mentors have different expertise, e.g. Miss X who is an experienced sports coach and has an interest in anti-racist work through involvement in sports.

The role of 'super' teaching assistant will be a big change. There will be difficulties in putting everyone into a new structure. We may have to do the Higher Level Teaching Assistant [HLTA] training. It will cause a lot of confusion. I don't know how everything connects together and there is no job description for the HLTA role yet. I don't know how it will work with existing job descriptions.

●●● Discussion

Most of the support staff had some 'history' with the school, for example many of the classroom assistants, teaching assistants, catering and cleaning staff and lunchtime organizers (previously known as 'dinner ladies') have had children at the school, either their own children or a relative's children. They have had a personal connection with the school and often have built up close relationships with staff and children before they come as members of staff. They also bring important and valuable knowledge and experience of the local area and the local community. Some started as cleaners and became teaching assistants. O'Brien and Garner (2001) identified three main reasons, from their discussions with support workers in schools, for choice of career: being a support worker in school enabled family responsibilities to be attended to in terms of convenience of timings and holidays; triggers such as positive or negative memories of one's own schooling; and serendipitous 'drifting into' becoming a volunteer helper in school and then being presented with an opportunity to formalize the involvement as a support worker. Many of the locally based support workers at Temple started off in this way. The personal connection sometimes is related to a parent's identification and experience of a child's special needs and seems to be a motivating factor for involvement in school, such as those described by the parent helper and the lunchtime organizer above.

The school also has a good record in funding and supporting all its staff members on appropriate and relevant training and development courses and events. These range from accredited courses to qualify as support workers, lunchtime organizers, teaching assistants and learning mentors through to master of education degrees (not only qualified teachers take these; support staff who have a first degrees are also eligible).

Many teachers and support workers have either experienced difficulty themselves or have children who have had difficulties too. This seems to be quite common occurrence, as Burke (2001) illustrates when he discusses his own experience of being at a school for children with moderate learning difficulties and how this experience helped him decide on a career as a learning support assistant in a special school. Another issue for some support workers is the decision whether to train as a teacher. There is some evidence to support the assertion that there is a growing number of teachers who begin their careers as support workers, undertake a part-time or full-time degree, if they do not already possess one, and then take one of the more flexible routes into teaching, such as the Graduate Teacher Programme which allows them to be trained in school with quasi-employment status and have a teaching commitment. The establishment of Foundation degrees in teaching and learning provides another possible route to qualification for support workers. By contrast, some support workers have no aspirations to become teachers, enjoying their different support roles in the classroom.

Contained within the report of the work of EMAS staff (see the bilingual instructor's story above) is an identification of improvement. The need to integrate EMAS work into the school's curriculum planning was one of the 'key issues' identified in the recent Ofsted report. Comments reflect significant work being done to see EMAS staff much more as similar to other staff rather than as 'outsiders' whose role is interventionist.

●●● Issues raised by the teachers and senior management team

This section explores the issues of partnership, management, playing to everyone's strengths, changing roles and culture as identified in the discussions with teachers and the senior management team. These are illustrated by quotations from the informal interviews.

Partnership with support staff

I do lots of team teaching with a whole variety of people: other teachers, bilingual instructors, EMAS teachers, teaching assistants, learning mentors and student teachers. I am always looking for more partnership strategies and researching ideas for development. I see my work with classroom support workers as a partnership. There is an important role in literacy development as teachers have a lot of knowledge and need to help others develop theirs. Support in this school is well organized and it works well in learning and in pastoral care. There is good leadership from the management team in school.

The senior management team share the responsibility for managing all the staff but some have a particular responsibility for groups of staff, e.g. the deputy head has the responsibility for managing the associate staff, their training, development and deployment.

We have in-house training as well as external training for all staff. The classroom team, people with different experience, also get some training together. In the classroom the teacher is still in charge. There is still a workload issue as we need more time for preparation, team planning and paperwork. We have an inclusive policy towards staff training and development. The management role should be about taking care, encouraging trust and responsibility amongst all staff.

Management issues

One of the biggest challenges is the management of such a diverse staff group. Some are not line managed by the senior management of the school but by the EMAS service, for example, and that can be difficult to handle when there are changes to be made. I want everyone to feel included. There is a great diversity of staff needs and you need to plan professional development to cope with different roles and differing abilities. The learning mentor team is a separate entity; they have a very specific brief, bringing about inclusion, and have very structured roles and undertake specific tasks. That can be difficult for one of the staff as she is 0.5 of the week as a learning mentor and 0.5 as a teaching assistant – a sort of split personality existence!

Playing to everyone's strengths

An important point about flexibility and focusing on the specific expertise of support staff is made below, and this highlights some of the differences in practice and roles between teachers and support workers:

Each member of the support team brings his or her own expertise. We try to get them to work to their own strengths. This is different from working with teachers. You can't afford for teachers not to have strengths in the core areas of maths and literacy but with support workers like Miss X you can use her expertise in sport and community work almost exclusively. You have a lot more flexibility about using the expertise of support workers. Learning mentors are attached to target children rather than a class. Sometimes these vulnerable children are linked to the team rather than one specific learning mentor and that means you have more flexibility to use the different strengths of the whole team.

Changing and evolving new roles

There are many challenges in the future as the workforce remodelling agenda is realized in schools, not least the changes that will happen as a new job is defined, especially that of the new higher-level teaching assistant. Even in a school where there have been many advances and developments in staff roles and responsibilities, there are feelings of apprehension and concern that financial and budgetary matters will cause problems and may not facilitate the best use of available staffing and may affect the quality of teaching in the school. There are, however, many opportunities for the development of innovative practices:

Another challenge facing the school is that of convincing those staff who were previously nursery nurses that they are perfectly capable of changing their role to that of teaching assistant. We are just about to begin looking at how we can use the performance management system to look at where there are skills gaps in our staffing base and then support people in developing and skilling people up. I am concerned about how we will cope with the remodelling of the workforce. It could be such a positive experience if we get it right. My biggest fear is that the early years staffing will suffer. We don't want to return to nursery officers running early years rather than teachers. It is often mentioned, by those who do not understand the importance of well qualified staff in the early years, that young children's behaviour is less challenging and staff don't need as high levels of subject knowledge as teachers in Key Stage 2, so therefore a school doesn't need teachers for young children. This would be a tragedy, especially as Foundation stage developments are just getting off the ground. On the other hand I have a teaching assistant who is very interested in history and she has been taking a Year 6 class for history and doing extremely well. Getting the right people in the right places is important. In the end the budget will determine what we do. It may not allow us to pay £19,000 to HLTAs.

Change in culture

As well as evolving new roles there was a recognition that the culture of the school, the accepted practices of the past and attitudes to work would have to change to facilitate the future developments in staff roles and responsibilities. The new roles would require closer working relationships between support and teaching staff to enable planning and evaluation:

There has got to be a change of culture and it won't happen overnight. Once teachers see that they can use their professional time more creatively and that it does not mean they have to leave their classrooms then they will choose to use their time differently. Many teachers would really like to have time to observe and assess children in depth. I think teachers should be allowed to organize their time in appropriate ways to suit them. When the staff members are all on different contracts it will be a real challenge to organize whole-staff training. At the moment we have support staff who start at 8.30 am and those who start at 10.00 am so they can run the after-school clubs.

●●● Discussion

There is little doubt that there will be challenges for all schools as they grapple with the remodelling of the workforce and the resultant changes in practice, culture, management and the structure of the school day for those who work in schools.

Nor must we forget the administrative staff, often seen as the glue that holds everything together in schools. This is true at Temple Primary School. The administrators have a good overall picture of a school and deal with the front-line services. They are often the first point of contact for parents, governors, teachers, children and visitors. There is very little that happens that is not known about 'in the office' where the bursar and secretary are both graduates. It is here that all deliveries, finances, telephones and correspondence are organized and recorded. There are implications for changes in roles for administrative staff as the size of the school staff increases and the need for effective communication becomes a priority. It is important to recognize that, for several years now, building up a top-class administrative and clerical support team has been a priority of the Governors' Personnel Subcommittee.

It is obvious that there has been a lot of development work with all staff to examine roles and responsibilities and that the management and organization of the staff (both teaching and support workers) has been subject to much discussion and consultation. A growing sense of the complexity of management structures that are required to manage such a diverse and multiprofessional staff is one of the significant issues arising from this small-scale investigation. Having staff in school managed by other services such as EMAS staff and caretaking and catering staff can cause tensions and requires creative and flexible management strategies. One defining feature of Temple Primary School is the commitment to consultation with all staff, governors, pupils and the local community. There is an ethos of partnership and collegiality in the school community that encompasses all its members and that aids the development of strategies to cope with a changing and evolving school context.

The composition of the governing body reflects a breadth and wealth of experience that may be unusual in primary schools: the chief executive of the council, local councillors who hold senior positions in the council, a former head of a university school of teacher education who chairs the regional teaching awards committee, a professor of education, a senior council officer, and more.

The issue of qualified staff in the early years of schooling is one that the senior management team feel strongly about, due to experience of working in this stage. The early years of schooling are arguably very important in forming good foundations for learning and for identifying individual needs that may require specialist support. Teachers who are highly skilled in assessment, diagnosis and planning appropriate activities to ensure development at this early stage are vital to children's early progress and success. Any moves to reduce qualified teacher involvement in the Foundation Stage will be seen by this school as an unacceptable feature of the implementation of the wider school workforce initiative. As a way of becoming more informed and having some influence in shaping local thinking, the headteacher has accepted a one day a week secondment to the LEA to investigate the issues for schools as they strive to implement the remodelling of the workforce initiative.

●●● What messages can we learn?

Drawing on the community

A school is more than its staff, pupils and buildings. The local community around Temple Primary School directly influences the pupils' lives and there is much to be gained from furthering closer interaction, links and liaison between school and community. The community is also a rich resource for support staff with valuable local knowledge and relevant skills.

Well developed staff development policies and practices

Having a good, transparent structure for all staff would seem to be an essential ingredient that supports policies and good practice in staff development. In a recent publication the promotion, planning and management of professional development for all staff members, teachers and support staff is recommended as good inclusive practice (Earley and Bubb, 2004).

Extensive consultation and 'talking through' of new ideas and initiatives

There is an expectation at Temple Primary School that staff will be consulted about developments. While this involves time and engagement from staff, the consequent ownership and engagement mean that staff invest enthusiasm and commitment in initiatives.

Square pegs in square holes

Getting the right staff in the right places can result in motivated staff gaining a real sense of achievement and progress and a degree of 'job satisfaction'.

Clear line management structures

This entails being sure that all staff know that they have a role in helping the children, who themselves are taught to respect every adult. It also entails knowing whom to go to for help, advice and resolution of difficult issues and policy decisions.

Budget problems if targeted funding ends

Like many schools that draw funds from short-term funding streams, the school is constantly aware of the budget problems that could arise when funding ceases. This could have serious implications for the staffing of the school, especially the number of support workers that could be employed.

Massive implications of workforce reforms

The as yet uncharted area of the implications of workforce reform and the effects on staff roles and responsibilities pose challenges for the management and deployment of staff. The secondment of the headteacher to the LEA to investigate the issues for primary schools will help the school stay in the forefront of developments.

Strong on emotional literacy

Keeping a staff engaged and 'on mission' and in touch with their relationships can create a strong learning community and a healthy attitude to change. A sense of being valued for one's contribution to the school and to children's learning and well-being helps build self-esteem throughout the school.

All different, all equal

An appreciation and celebration of the different individual cultural, linguistic and learning backgrounds of children and adults help promote an acceptance and understanding of diversity and promote inclusive practices.

●●● References

Burke, S. (2001) 'Spencer's story: it's all about learning', in T. O'Brien, and P. Garner, (eds) *Untold Stories: Learning Support Assistants and their Work*. Stoke-on-Trent: Trentham Books.

Campbell, A. and Kane, I. (1998) *School-based Teacher Education: Telling Tales from a Fictional Primary School*. London: David Fulton.

Cooper, H. and Hyland, R. (eds) (2000) *Children's Perceptions of Learning with Trainee Teachers*. London: RoutledgeFalmer.

Earley, P. and Bubb, S. (2004) *Leading and Managing Continuing Professional Development: Developing People, Developing Schools*. London: Paul Chapman Publishing.

O'Brien, T. and Garner, P. (eds) (2001) *Untold Stories: Learning Support Assistants and their Work*. Stoke-on-Trent: Trentham Books.

●●● Chapter 10

Peering into the future: two conversations with headteachers

Anne Campbell

This chapter seeks to bring our discussion of support workers up to date, by placing in it the context of current workforce reform, which is itself an ongoing and unfinished exercise. It is based on two interviews with headteachers in different local education authorities (LEAs), Angela and Barbara (fictitious names), who were seconded to work on workforce remodelling with their LEAs. Angela was on a full-time secondment to implement and manage the remodelling initiative in her LEA. She had had three headships and, in her last one, had brought a school out of special measures. Barbara was seconded with a colleague for one day per week to find out what headteachers in the LEA thought about the initiative. The purpose of the interviews was to discover the realities of school life during the current stages of the remodelling process.

Following the earlier chapters where individual roles have been explored and discussed, it seemed necessary to gather some information about how individual roles would change. The workforce remodelling is a major government initiative (see www.teachernet.gov.uk/wholeschool/remodelling for a comprehensive update involving radical and, at times, controversial changes in schools; see also www.remodelling.org.uk).

Some answers to the following key questions were sought:

- What does the remodelling of the workforce initiative look like?
- What changes are being made to support roles?
- What are the problems facing schools and LEAs in the challenges of remodelling the workforce?
- What are the political and union issues surrounding support in the classroom?

●●● Interview with Angela

Question: Why did you take this role after three headships?

Angela: Here was a chance to use one of the schools' most valuable aspects – the community around. Workforce reforms were about the needs of the pupils, delivering in different ways, enabling different groupings, a flexibility which would help the support staff with targeted work, looking at the resource that parents would bring to school, and perhaps looking then at future employees in the school who were part of the community. There is a social dimension to workforce reforms: there are young women whose children are now at school, and so what can they offer us and we offer them? Mum becomes a dinner lady, and then perhaps goes on to some classroom support and then realizes that she's exceptionally good at this. In a good school she would be nurtured, extended, provided for. I've seen people come up like that and go on to be excellent teachers. Someone once said that if we always do what we always did then we'll always get what we always got. In some schools that might be alright, but the children are moving into a different world.

Question: Workforce reform – is it driven by teachers?

Angela: It is, and I'm a teacher and a practitioner, but if it was about recruiting more teachers or making life easier, if that was where it had stopped, then I wouldn't have been interested. However, I don't see it stopping there. I agree that if you get a teacher or any member of school staff who has had a restful weekend or has got work life balance, they bring enthusiasm back into school. If you've got teachers and other staff who work in a school who are exhausted, ground down by all the things that go on, then they're not likely to be interesting teachers or people to be with children – that's the bottom line.

Question: What is your role?

Angela: I am the workforce remodelling adviser for the LEA. I organize events; I help to roll out the national programme about remodelling, and about delivering the contractual agreements. It's also about managing change, and here the national remodelling team's model of change through the National College of School Leadership is an integral part. So part of my job is to promote the change management model; it's also to work with individual schools focusing in on what the children are getting out of it and about good practice and staff development. My job's really diverse. Some of it is training, some of it is work with individual heads; I also liase with six or seven other local authorities, some of which are part of a federation of LEAs who work together on remodelling.

Question: How do you connect with the national remodelling team?

Angela: They visit regionally and over the last six months we have had fairly regular half-termly meetings. There is now a regional national remodelling team adviser who visits all the regional co-ordinators. I've also been working on job descriptions, looking at pay scales, looking at good practice, working also with the LEA co-ordinator for teaching assistants. I do a lot of training for them and am working on plans for higher-level teaching assistant [HLTA] programmes. We've just put together a job description for a HLTA; we've also put together some guidance about how you may use staff other than teachers to cover classes, and I also liaise with the unions and try and reconcile problems.

Question: What issues are there with the unions?

Angela: The National Union of Teachers [NUT] nationally and locally have a line – no one other than teachers should be taking classes or covering for planning, preparation and assessment [PPA] time.

I don't agree with it, but I respect it. In the past there were times when I would have support staff for cover, always with teachers' agreement; sometimes they would say that they would rather have a teaching assistant cover, rather than a supply teacher 'off the street' who doesn't know anything about the children. Even with the best systems in the world you couldn't give a supply teacher knowledge about particular children if they were only doing a one-day cover. My judgement was always based on what is best for the children as well as what's best for the staff. Even before the workforce reforms we looked at a system of honoraria in schools. I couldn't pay my support staff as teachers, but what I could say at the end of the term is here is a token of how much we value what you do. It was working quite well.

Question: Are there any special issues with headteacher unions in particular? The National Association of Head Teachers and Secondary Headteachers' Association [NAHT and SHA]?

Angela: Money. I deal also with secondary heads through a very mixed group called a Workforce Agreement Monitoring Group [WAMG] that's made up nationally of representatives of the signatories so it excludes the NUT. We have a local WAMG: UNISON, PAT, NUSWT and ATL. We also have SHA and NAHT and a representative from a group of secondary headteachers, a governor, a school improvement officer, myself, my secretary and some LEA human resources personnel. Some of us always attend but others dip in and dip out. Money, I think, is the big one with headteachers. I think the secondary schools are different in terms of the 2005 contractual agreement because of the tradition of 'free periods'. Although many primary schools have been able to give some release time, there aren't many that have given planning, preparation and assessment time as an entitlement. In primary schools there are many more questions.

Question: Any issues with UNISON?

Angela: Our local UNISON is very concerned and the regional officer comes sometimes. I do have another working group specifically on aspects of the support staff: pay, conditions and job description. Their main concern is the speed at which expectations have been delivered. I think that many people thought that there would have been faster progress for support staff, but consultation takes a long time. There are concerns around conditions of service.

May we just talk about maybe classroom support at the moment and leave aside admin officers and ICT technicians? In the context of classroom support you've got nursery nurses who have worked in different conditions of service so they've been paid 32 hours over 52 weeks, and they've had a status that they consider is a higher level than a classroom assistant because you can come into classroom assistant level with no recognized qualifications. UNISON have stressed those worries but it would be financially impossible for schools and local authorities to move all support staff to the paid conditions of teachers for 52 weeks of the year working 195 days. So what we tried to do in our LEA was to bring the nursery nurses into the new job descriptions for the teaching assistant levels and show that by moving into, say, T3, there was a career progression. At the moment most nursery nurses just go up to point 15 and that's where they stay. Now they would have access to higher points. Working and being paid term time only with less hours in a week, they could still gain about £100 a year. More important is the access to the higher levels. We were successful at selling that to nursery nurses. The question came up about the effect on pensions. None the less, we've now produced some LEA proposals that say if nursery nurses want to stay as they are then that's fine.

There were other issues that UNISON were concerned about such as the move to job evaluation by all the LEAs. When job evaluation comes there may be some mismatch involving those jobs that have 'add ons'. If you have a special support assistant working in a specialist school they may have a supplement or have additional pay if they have a qualification. Such things will disappear with job evaluation. To remodel taking account of something that was to come later, was one step too far.

Question: What are the LEA's main objectives?

Angela: I think there are two main objectives: one is to comply with the expecta-tions of the DfES about a proper career structure. It isn't just about teachers. UNISON and GMB didn't sign up to make teachers lives easier; they signed up to make support staff more valued, to have better pay and conditions and to give career paths. The second objective was to try and provide some models of good practice. It's in our interest to start remodelling and get some consistency. So we've been looking at how we monitor, how we gather good practice which is transferable.

Question: Is remodelling going to reduce bureaucracy?

Angela: There's no sign of that at the moment. However if we still have the same amount of bureaucracy in three years' time, I would be worried, but I think that successful change isn't stopping one thing and starting another, I think it's where you move two things together. On a very practical level, they used to call it pump priming. You need to gradually reduce what you've got. What I think schools are not doing enough of is questioning what they do not need to do. In the beginning of anything new, you really do need paper. I found that under 'special measures' – but not for ever. We need to ask ourselves at the end of each academic school year, what do we still need to do and why? I think that's the case with workforce reform. We're going to need a lot of paper knowledge about what you can and can't do, but if we're still relying on that paper knowledge, still filling in countless bits of paper in three years time, then it's gone wrong.

Question: What about time for planning, preparation and assessment [PPA]?

Angela: I think that even if you didn't bring workforce reforms in you should still have some dedicated planning and assessment time with your teaching assis-tant. I think that's separate to teachers' general PPA time because, if I were a head, I would want to see the way that teachers use their planning, preparation and assessment time. But as a teacher I've got half a day now, I can go through all that software that we got through e-learning credits, or to go and look at, say, that group of boys whose writing isn't very good, I need to give them things to start them off. So there needs to be PPA time with teaching assistants and PPA time for researching new initiatives. I think most primary schools have been steadily getting better at this.

Question: What would you summarize as the key issues regarding teaching assistants?

Angela: You must distinguish between the teaching assistant as the person who is covering and taking the class, and then the teaching assistant working alongside the teacher. These are two distinct roles. Not every teaching assistant will want to take a class, and the teacher has got to be the one who specifies the work within the National Curriculum. I think that is not fully understood in schools yet. A teacher would expect a teaching assistant regularly working with a group of children to know what their learning needs were.

Question: What is the role of higher-level teaching assistants [HLTAs]?

Angela: Well, we've got some HLTAs who did the pilot last year. In the job descriptions we don't see them as being the ones who just cover the classes; we see them as having a high-level input, either as part of the team or maybe delivering to a class while the teacher takes a small group for more focused work. We don't see it that the HLTA will be the one who is the substitute teacher.

Question: What are the TA levels envisaged?

Angela: We've looked at four levels, starting at TA1, which is a fairly low level of interaction with the children. It could be somebody getting things ready in the classroom, sitting with a group of children perhaps just to keep them on task. The next level is TA2 which should involve more independence and interaction with the children. TA3 is where we feel the nursery nurses will fit in, and that might also be where your HLTA in terms of salary fits in. Then you have TA4 – this is equivalent to a newly qualified teacher with a high level of independence, and they might have a managerial responsibility of other TAs.

TA2s are the lowest level we envisage taking a class. For TA1 there might be some supervision – a small group that you could take to the library but not taking the class for any length of time. Only in an emergency would a TA1 take over, but sometimes the individual skills that a person has are not reflected in their salary.

It's complex. There are times when teachers desperately need someone to do 'photocopying' and a TA might be paid for admin half the time but be required to act as a cover. The TA might have the skills and qualifications and experience, so afternoons might be spent as a TA3 and mornings as a TA1. Our LEA has 'specific purpose' contracts where TA is attached to an individual child. They may be attached in the morning for personal care needs, but in the afternoon, because they have lots of experience, might be used as a TA3.

Question: So, summing up, which groups have worries about workforce reform?

Angela: I've said nursery nurses over the years have felt that their role is being undermined; the other thing is that nobody now advertises for a nursery nurse. They advertise for a TA because a lot of people are qualified by experience rather than qualifications. I could include some teaching staff on the worry list – for example one of my teachers said: 'I didn't come into this profession to have half a day a week off.' My job was to persuade her that to have the afternoon off to learn other skills, she could develop and become an even better teacher.

There are some teachers who feel exposed when somebody else goes into their classroom, and so there are some teachers who are never absent because they don't want anyone else in their classroom because it maybe exposes a lack of organization. Other teachers are ultra-organized and don't like someone else's perceived lower standards. While it quite excites me that every school will have its own solution it's actually quite frightening. A number of headteachers have simply said to me: 'Tell me how to do it!' A range of people are feeling uncomfortable.

Question: What are the main benefits to schools?

Angela: Those schools that have not in the past included all staff in their decision-making now have a brilliant opportunity to do so. The notion of the 'quick fix' is often very good; there are some things that you can do very quickly that create a more positive motivational climate. Schools will also have a 'grow your own' capacity: bring people into your school and they become involved with all the school values. There's also a positive message going out to the children with the utilization of different skills. There are many benefits, and I think for headteachers it is the opportunity for them not to be the solution bringers, which can be quite threatening but it can also be quite exhilarating.

Question: Where will the money come from?

Angela: It's not going to come from the LEA; it'll have to come from the government. What I said to the schools that I work with is that I think you can often do it without money: you can make economies of scale and some things you could do as a federation or as a group of schools. I think that the government will put money in but unless they do it obviously, schools may not see it. There's been a move to deliver everything through pupil numbers. That would be a disaster in primary schools because the pupil numbers are contracting. You've only go to lose one family – three children – and you might be £6,000 down. That's the real dilemma in terms of money. If extra money came and you could straightaway employ an extra teacher, when you haven't gone through the thinking then effectively the money's disappeared. New money should be ring fenced and protected – a pot of money you can have for the next three years regardless of how the numbers change. That would make a huge difference.

The NAHT say that they need to know by December 2005 otherwise they're pulling out of the agreement, so does UNISON – they say they'll pull out, but the bottom line is that it's still contractual.

●●● Interview with Barbara

Question: What is your seconded role?

Barbara: A colleague and myself were approached by the LEA to see if we'd be interested in a one day per week secondment looking at workforce remodelling from the point of view of headteachers and schools. The LEA could see that heads were becoming aware of the policy position of the government through the training programme, but they weren't too sure about exactly what was going on at ground level.

Question: Has the role changed as you've gone on?

Barbara: It has changed. Our brief was to visit schools one day a week. There was a lot of uncertainty in the early days and one of the tasks was to try to find out what creative thought was going on. Were people thinking out of the box? We picked up on quite a lot of negatives at the outset as people were very unclear. We were put out there at a very early stage and some heads and deputies hadn't had the training. Latterly we've encountered different thinking. Heads have taken things a lot further, no longer just dabbling.

Question: So what are the current issues?

Barbara: The first issue was the tasks. Last September teachers withdrew from a number of tasks. I think the unions and headteachers expected difficulties. I think that process has gone remarkably smoothly probably due to the fact that a lot of headteachers and senior leadership teams had moved some things already, for instance, collection of dinner monies. A few years ago, most teaching staff stopped collecting money and administration hours were increased. Administrative salaries were increased in line and so the collection of dinner money and school fund money and similar things wasn't really as much of an issue. Exam invigilation was not really relevant to primary schools, although I did wonder whether the SATs might cause problems. In fact a lot of heads have reported that their Year 6 teachers have said in effect: 'If you think I've taught this Year 6 class for the whole year and I'm not actually going to sit there and give them encouraging looks and smile at them on the day you can forget it.'

I thought 'display of work' would be a big one. A lot of teachers have resisted that with, 'We've put the work into this; we want to display it', so staff and heads have come to a negotiated conclusion. If the teacher wants to do the display then the teacher can, but if teachers want to withdraw then let them withdraw and train teaching assistants to do it. So I think the tasks have worked out well.

The big issue that everybody's worried about is the 'cover' issue from September 2004, because from 2004 teachers should only cover 38 hours a year. Problems will arise, apart from the obvious one of having the right people to cover. There's also a big bureaucratic task of keeping timesheets and more for each member of staff so you know exactly how many hours they have worked over the year. That increases bureaucracy, and is going to be a difficult one. There is the fundamental issue of teaching assistants' having the right knowledge and the ability to take classes. Heads have commented in schools in difficult areas: 'It's hard for my deputy head to manage behaviour in Year 6. How's a teaching assistant going to do it?' Now obviously there are two sides to that and the training is crucial.

The other thing that's probably the greatest concern is the PPA time. In September 2005 every teacher requires planning, preparation and assessment time and it's got to be 10 per cent of their normal timetable even if they're part time. If they are, for example, a special needs co-ordinator (.5 timetabled and .5 special needs), it's still 10 per cent of the total amount, so that's going to be a huge burden for staffing budgets. The advice that we're getting from the education department and the message we're spreading across the authority is that schools need to have a go at the PPA time this year – perhaps look at cover for the first term and start introducing PPA time; for some schools that won't necessarily be an issue, because those schools have a lot of non-contact time anyway. Secondary schools aren't seeing PPA as a challenge at all but, certainly, for small primary schools it is going to be significant.

Question: What are the teachers' unions saying?

Barbara: I don't think anything significant has come up yet and the tasks were resolved easily; I think that probably took the unions by surprise. I think the unions really will start looking closely when the cover requirement comes in; I think later there'll be more issues. The unions are all signed up to the agreement apart from the NUT and are working together on it. There are some issues that

I've been surprised have got through: for instance the national workforce remodelling team has produced all these wretched timesheets and that's a bureaucratic nightmare when we're trying to reduce paperwork. I know in theory you can do it all through IT but even so you've still got to input the data. I do think things will start to get a bit hot. There's bound to be a case where a teacher is asked to cover for longer than 38 hours – because cover isn't just a question of covering a whole class. If you actually take one child and put it in a class as an extra that is defined as cover, so splitting classes can't happen, and a lot of schools do that at the moment.

Question: Any issues coming up from UNISON, who represent the support workers?

Barbara: They've signed up to the agreement. I'm not aware of anything. There's an issue with nursery nurses which has been a big problem. Their NNEB qualification hasn't actually been recognized, so consequently they feel devalued. In terms of pay scales and levels, heads have struggled to work out where to put NNEBs and I know that UNISON have been involved across the country where they've felt that there's been unfair treatment.

Question: How's the LEA organizing the 'sorting out' of definitions of status, job descriptions and salary levels for teaching assistants?

Barbara: Our LEA was ahead of the game and they produced salary grades last financial year. We were all trained to situate our teaching assistants. We had meetings with the teaching assistants; we were given a draft framework of job descriptions. We were asked to meet with teaching assistants individually to interview them about their future and then they were invited to say, almost like a bid, where they felt they were in that framework. Then the information was assimilated in terms of pay. Heads met with their finance subcommittees and/or the governing body to finalize things. In many schools it worked absolutely fine; staff commented on exactly what they did, where they thought they should be and were assimilated. However, since then the government's workforce remodelling team has brought out new job description frameworks, and the gradings don't coincide with the LEA ones, so my fellow seconded colleague and I are now looking at trying to adjust the local gradings to the proposed national gradings.

One of the issues that's come out is that the national grading appears to be channelling teaching assistants down certain avenues: there are job descriptions for curriculum, job descriptions for managing learning, and job descriptions for behaviour management. Our brief at the moment between now and the end of term is to try and write draft job descriptions for the different levels for teaching assistants locally. That's come up as a request from heads. I think heads have reached the point where they actually want the LEA to say, 'Right, do this, put some on a TA2, put others on a TA1 higher, put those on a TA3' and so on.

One interesting thing we've picked up is the difference in terms of special needs support. We've got some schools and some heads who believe that because you're supporting a special needs child it takes a certain kind of personality and a certain kind of knowledge and a certain character – so they will pay their one-to-one special needs support at a high rate, whereas there are other schools that are saying, 'Well, hang on, they're only working one to one, so they should be on a lower rate'. There are disparities right away, right through the authority on that.

Question: The scale begins with the TA1. Is that right?

Barbara: There's the TA1 lower and a TA1 higher, TA2, TA3 and TA4 in the local scheme but in the national scheme it goes up to 5.

Question: So, take the TA1 lower. Is that somebody who just does basic things in support?

Barbara: It's a support role but without it being a general office admin role. It's preparing materials, it's photocopying, it's washing the paint pots, working totally under the direction of the class teacher.

Question: The TA1 higher?

Barbara: Here you're starting to provide one-to-one support with children, maybe a couple of children, still under the direction of the class teacher. TA2 involves working with a group, still under the direction of the teacher, and then TA3 is moving to whole-class work, again still under the direction of the teacher. As to TA4 – there's a bit of a disagreement between what's whole class and what isn't and I think the unions may be pushing for a TA4 to be the HLTA standard where you take a whole class. But the LEA's position at the moment is that TA3 is higher-level teaching assistant [HLTA] status because, of course, the one thing that we haven't got in all of this is any extra funding.

Question: We'll come to that later.

Barbara: OK.

Question: In my conversation with Angela, she thought the HLTAs were on TA3 along with nursery nurses?

Barbara: Yes, that's what we're looking at, although some nursery nurses were assimilated to TA2.

Question: She only spoke of four grades: TA1 which was the basic one, TA2 a little more interaction, TA3 nursery nurses, 'for instance', TA4 more managerial, no reference to a 5 at all. The position between LEAs seems very variable.

Barbara: Quite, and that's an issue in itself, and the learning mentors are another strand. Where do you put the learning mentors because learning mentor co-ordinators have been paid really quite high up that scale, and yet they haven't worked with whole classes? They've been working with specific groups of children, but they are our most vulnerable children. Therefore they are more challenging.

Question: Right, let's come to why we're doing all this. What are seen as the benefits?

Barbara: There's a point of view that we're doing it because we've got a recruitment crisis coming up. I can't remember the exact figures but it's significant. Something like 50 per cent of the workforce is over 40. In our LEA, it's actually higher. There are huge fears that we're not actually going to be able to recruit enough teachers. Therefore one of the ways of fast tracking into the profession is through the HLTA, and the government are currently planning professional development for HLTAs to get QTS status. That is the cynical approach. The other side is that, according to research, teachers were actually teaching for only a minority of the school day and it's quite true. If you separate out the teaching, which after all is the job we are trained for, there's actually also a large chunk on admin, registration, sorting out problems, sorting out behaviour things during lunch. So the benefits to the school would be that teachers could do the job that they are paid to do and should be doing.

There are also huge benefits for the teaching assistants and I feel very strongly about this because there are teaching assistants at a range of levels and I don't mean levels in terms of payment levels or grades, I mean in terms of their experience, their enthusiasm, the experience they've brought to the job. This will give them a structure to be able to develop. At our school we've been doing performance management for our associate staff and we're at the end of our second cycle. The exercise demonstrates that they are valued. The fact that we call them associate staff as opposed to teaching assistants or non-teachers is in itself saying that we value them. Very often children will tell teaching assistants things that they might not actually share with the teacher. So I think they are a very valuable resource. They've been underestimated and I think this will actually put them on the map and say here is a group of people who are very good, who deserve professional development.

I know the national group is now looking at professional development right from TA1. The government's bringing in different packages, because there's been very little training available for them. They could do the NVQ Level 1 and Level 2, but after that there's been nothing. I've got associate staff who are keen to do more, but are trapped. But we've got to remember that there are some teaching assistants who came in to support work because they wanted to help children in the classroom, and they don't want to become teachers. We've got to respect that.

Question: What are the problems, then?

Barbara: The bureaucracy is certainly a concern. So is recognizing that not all TAs want to be teachers. I anticipate there'll be problems in terms of who's going to go through to HLTA status. There was only one person in our school who was able to access the pilot HLTA training because she had her maths and English GCSE. So straightaway you're discounting a lot of staff and there is an argument that 15 years working in Reception or Nursery as a former nursery nurse is as valuable as an English and maths GCSE to some schools in the early years. So I think there'll be a problem if governing bodies are dogmatic and insist on maths and English GCSEs without recognizing them in other ways status-wise. Core skills Level 2 is a good alternative.

Question: Let's talk a little bit about HLTAs and the concept of that role.

Barbara: We've been asked to nominate HLTAs for training but that's a marathon job for the authority and very costly. It's also going to be very difficult because there aren't many qualified or verified trainers. So we're looking at present in the LEA at how we can encourage staff to apply for HLTA status. One of the things we are trying to roll out across the authority is extra maths lessons for teaching assistants in the evening. The authority have funded those and that's been very successful, so I've had, I think, it's 18 teaching assistants who've had ten lessons with the maths teacher from the local high school and that's been very good for them and they're going to be taking their maths exam in the next few weeks. If they get that, they will then be able to access the HLTA training.

However, there's still a considerable gap between what they are experiencing on the HLTA training and traditional qualified teacher status. Yet these HLTAs are going to be used as supply staff to do cover, to do the PPA time. I'm not convinced from what I've seen so far that the training is enough for them, although I think training on the job is extremely powerful. These HLTAs can't be put into classrooms and told to get on with it because that will fail. They're going to need considerable support. Their work is supposed to be under the direction of the class teacher, but if the class teacher isn't there on the Monday morning because they've phoned in sick then you've got an issue.

Question: What about the time needed by teachers for planning and preparation conferences? Doesn't this add to the workload?

Barbara: That is going to a challenge. Again I think in a large primary school there are ways round it because you can plan alongside your year group colleague and your HLTA could come in on Monday morning and get the information from the year group colleague. Yes, there are issues for planning. In 2005 you'll be given time for your planning so maybe by 2005 it'll be a more positive experience for people but at the moment in terms of just the cover if you've got to leave everything ready for the class and then you've also got to get feedback from the HLTA afterwards then it could be seen as more, not less, work. On the other hand, if members of staff can get quality time out of the classroom – if they go on a course and they can be relaxed on the course because they are confident the person who is in their class is somebody that the children know – then that's got to be a positive.

Question: Who will be evaluating performance?

Barbara: The headteachers and senior staff I presume, because the only sort of line in the agreement is that heads can put members of staff in charge of classes provided they feel that they have got the necessary experience and qualifications. You don't have to use a HLTA – I could put anybody in front of a class providing I felt that they could cope and that it would benefit the children. So I believe that it will be senior leadership teams in schools evaluating it, but there's much work still to be undertaken. Where a school's vision and the ethos are established and it's all up and running and staff communication is good then I think this is going to be a positive development, but where, perhaps, there are problems that already exist in the school then it could add to them.

Question: OK, let's talk money again.

Barbara: The information I've got on this is that there isn't any. In one sense there has been money already. I think money's been given to the authority and used for secondments and training. The training's been fantastic in our LEA. Every head and every deputy head has had at least two or three sessions and there's more to come. There's a lot of money gone in now for the 'tranche' sessions, where you go for two days and you do the paper exercises all about change management. I'm doing it in October (2004).

Question: Doing what exactly?

Barbara: We get intensive training for change management, ready for the workforce remodelling. One of the things we've asked for and it's agreed, is to put deputies on as well, because it's got to be a team effort. In terms of other money, we live in hope that something will come in April 2005 for the next financial year in order to tackle PPA because that can't be done without money. There's quite a strong feeling that, if money isn't available, the unions may withdraw, particularly the NAHT. But nobody's actually told us what the money is and whether it's going to be new money. The concerns are that there will be money but it will be Standards Fund money or project money which will have been recycled from another pot.

Question: Isn't it contractual already?

Barbara: The PPA? It is contractual, yes, so how we would withdraw I don't know.

Question: Have you got any stories you want to talk around?

Barbara: There are some interesting things going on. One school closes early on a Friday afternoon and all the children are invited to take part in extra-curricular activities clubs – so they're not doing clubs Monday to Thursday lunchtime or after school. They put all that into the Friday afternoon. Teaching assistants and any volunteers run those clubs while all the teachers plan together. That's another issue that I've not mentioned about the PPA time – very good idea in essence, ideally if you're going to release all your staff at once, because staff want to plan together. That's difficult unless you do close the school early like I cited. Another school is closing on a Friday and the children are doing similar sorts of activities and they've introduced the music service, sports coaches, anybody and everybody, anybody warm and willing comes in to take the children.

One thing we haven't talked about at all is parents' perceptions of workforce reform. I think we're going to have to do a lot of marketing convincing parents that a child is in just as good hands with a teaching assistant as with a teacher. I think that could become a problem in some schools.

Other things I've picked up on? One thing that we're doing ourselves which has been very positive, is sports coaches – we've got a team of sports coaches who come in and help at lunchtime. That's helped the behaviour. What we have recognized with workforce remodelling is it's not just about HLTAs, it's about looking at the whole school, and who's best deployed where. We decided we'd put more money into sports coaches and less money into lunchtime organizers, remodelling the workforce in that way.

One of the benefits of going round to other schools is that you're a fresh face and you look at a person's school in a different light and in one particular school the head said: 'I just don't know how I'm going to try and release my teaching staff; it's a big school and I want them to be released together so I want the two Year 6 teachers to plan together in 2005; but how can I do that?' When she actually took me round the school we realized that some of the walls were partitions and one way of doing it was actually pulling the partition back and both year 6 classes being with two teaching assistants, possibly three teaching assistants. In that way, you can release two teachers at the same time. So there are different ways round things and people are starting to think more creatively and more positively.

Question: So it's definitely going to happen then, 'because it's contractual'?
Barbara: Yes.

Question: So, ten years on what do you see as the big changes in schools?
Barbara: Well, possibly there'll be fewer teachers or we'll have this new breed of teachers who've come through HLTA into QTS via a fast track. How good they'll be I don't know because we haven't seen the training yet, but I hope that it's a good package otherwise it would be unfair on the children and unfair on the staff. I certainly see that teaching assistants will start to develop down different avenues. You'll get some people who are curriculum orientated and they'll be helping the intervention strategies, assuming we've still got intervention strategies in ten years. Then I think there will be teaching assistants who have trained purely in behaviour management and then I think there will be teaching assistants who are specifically supporting administrative tasks, helping teachers with the photocopying and the classroom materials and preparation.

I think the traditional role of a teaching assistant who 'belongs' to a teacher or a teaching assistant who 'belongs' to a group of pupils will have gone. I'm hoping that there will be less stress in the workforce, I'm hoping that we'll retain staff as a result of that. Apparently, there's a big problem with NQTs leaving in their first and second year and hopefully if they're given quality planning and preparation time they won't feel as stressed; if they've got time to do some of the marking, some of the preparation then they won't be working all the hours at home. Hopefully we will have a more positive team approach to teaching.

Question: Anything else you want to add?
Barbara: I think I've covered everything. We've all been asked to set up change management teams and some schools have done this. In my school we asked who wanted to be on the change management team and every single member of the support staff wanted to be on it, so that completely defeated the object – but

that just shows how insecure people feel at the moment about the process. Everybody wants to be involved in it at the highest level, in order to sort of keep their eye on it. But, 'change management team' is the government buzz phrase for moving plans forward.

●●● Issues, questions and dilemmas in the context of workforce remodelling

The two interviews have raised many issues, questions and dilemmas, which could provide an agenda for discussion for staff development days and governors' meetings. These issues and questions are first organized into groups. A selection of the key ones will be addressed and discussed further in Chapter 11. It is useful to remind ourselves that the two headteachers had different perspectives: Angela was concerned about how to make it work generally, and Barbara focused on the impact on schools from a headteacher's view.

Roles and job descriptions

Issues
- There would appear to be different roles for TAs, not just different grades, and a need for a national career structure for associate staff.
- Classroom teachers will lose their close relationship with a particular TA.
- There could be rough water ahead when job evaluation 'kicks in' and anomalies appear.
- There is no sign of a national agreement on grades.

Questions
- What will the new status of the nursery nurse be?
- Where do learning mentors, learning support assistants, second language instructors, mixed 'special purpose' assistants and similar anomalies fit in?
- What exactly is a HLTA?
- Who will evaluate the new jobs/roles and the use of TAs to take classes?

Change and management of workloads

Issues
- The remodelling is an exercise in change management – but a 'right' model seems to have been handed down.
- Remodelling is increasing teachers' workloads as they 'direct' TAs, not reducing them. More conference time is needed.
- Change is tougher for primary schools, certainly the provision of cover for PPA.

Questions
- Will the outcome in a school be through staff consensus or need resolving by headteacher 'diktat', or possibly LEA formula advice?
- Will TAs always be under the direction of teachers?
- Will monitoring cover cause more bureaucracy?

Community, parents and the social dimension of remodelling

Issues
- Involving members of the community more as TAs may cause ethical issues about delicate and sensitive data on individuals.
- This initiative is not just about teachers, and this may not be widely appreciated.

Questions
- What kind of opportunities will workforce remodelling provide for the community?
- What attitudes will parents have to their children being taught by TAs? Or to schools having lesson-free days? How will these ideas be marketed to parents?

Training and professional development

Issues
- On-the-job training can often be 'cheap' training.
- There will be a new employment route into teaching for HLTAs.
- TAs need a good level of subject knowledge to teach subjects.

Questions
- Will classroom teachers need training to manage and direct TAs?
- What will the HLTA training look like after the pilots?
- What would a HLTA have to do to gain QTS?
- Would trainee teachers be trained how to work with TAs and HLTAs?
- Will the training be enough or good enough, or is it the Mum's Army with a certificate?

Money, money, money

Issues
- Schools may have to choose between the budget options of having one experienced teacher or two HLTAs or extended use of other TAs.
- Creative approaches to staffing may develop a more flexible workforce with a blurring of boundaries between teachers and teaching assistants.
- Teachers should have more time to teach – the task they are in theory paid for.

Questions
- Where will the money come from? Will that money for teaching assistants have to be taken from an existing pot?
- Is the money really necessary to remodel the workforce?

And, finally, in controversial mode, one comment could be in response to all the issues and questions: 'It's contractual so it will happen.' As this book goes to press, the jury is very much still out on much of the foregoing.

Chapter 11

Developing successful practice with support staff

Anne Campbell

In this chapter I identify and discuss key issues and features from the previous chapters in the book, from research done for a recent dissertation (Randall, 2004) and from the current debates around workforce reform. They will provide guidance and support for developing successful practice when working collaboratively with voluntary support assistants, learning mentors, nursery nurses, students, teaching assistants and special needs assistants. The chapter draws conclusions and hopefully suggests a set of practices that bring together ideas developed in each of the chapters about roles, responsibilities and ways to develop collaborative practice.

●●● Let a thousand flowers bloom?

One of the major issues arising from this book is the need to understand the complexity and range of support roles in schools and classrooms. This book could therefore have been subtitled 'Let a thousand flowers bloom', indicating the plethora of named support roles. Nomenclature is a major area of controversy. What support workers are called is important but, due to the previous use of different job titles such as nursery nurse, classroom assistant, teaching assistant and learning support assistant, can also be confusing. Complicating the area even more are the differing training, status, conditions of service, job descriptions and pay of the various support workers in school. Nursery nurses arguably have had good cause to be aggrieved when their title and status were changed to teaching assistants, as they were the group of support workers who had the longest and most vocationally orientated training while others, such as classroom assistants, could be parent helpers with no formal training. Conversely some classroom assistants, are very well qualified, some having degrees including highly relevant degrees in education studies, early years studies or psychology as well as a qualification for support assistants. Similarly, learning support assistants for children with special educational needs have varying levels of qualifications, expertise and experience. Learning mentors pose similar issues. Many learning mentors have degree-level qualifications in relevant areas such as social work, community studies and education and are paid at entry to teaching level of salary.

As many LEAs have found as they embark on trying to construct job descriptions and pay scales for the diverse workforce of school support workers, this is a minefield, fraught with histories of past roles, varying customs and practices in schools, residential care and private and voluntary sector involvement. As can be gleaned from the two headteachers in Chapter 10, there are varying practices across different LEAs with regard to job descriptions and pay scales. This makes the national picture complex and difficult to manage centrally.

It has been useful in this book to map and explore the development of roles and functions of people other than qualified teachers in classrooms. The term 'support worker' has been used throughout this book as a general term but it covers the following roles: the now defunct nursery nurse; the member of the community; the parent or grandparent helper; the learning support assistant for children with special educational needs; the learning mentor; the teaching assistant; the student teacher; the bilingual support worker/teacher/instructor depending on his or her qualifications; and, arguably in the near future, possibly the most controversial of all the roles, the large number of higher-level teaching assistants (HLTA) to be employed in schools. In the future all support workers will be called teaching assistants. As pointed out in Chapter 10, there are two distinct strands to the roles: those teaching assistants who are covering and taking the class; and the teaching assistants working alongside the teacher. Other distinctions are emerging too. Do teaching assistants support the teacher or the child? Or is the important distinction support in the classroom or across the school? Or is it all these? The main areas of support can be listed as: curriculum support as in literacy, numeracy and ICT; behaviour support as linked to learning mentors' work; administrative support (e.g. for photocopying and dinner-money collection); classroom support (such as mounting displays and cleaning art and technology areas and tools); and pupil support for children with special educational needs or for specific group activities. The importance of definition of role is an important one which, as recognized in many of the chapters, normally requires individual, personalized negotiation. Not every teaching assistant will want to take a class, and the teacher has got to be the one who specifies the work within the National Curriculum

The role of the nursery nurse serves as a good example to explore the impact of changes in government policies on support workers in schools in the last ten years. Nursery nurses have seen substantive changes in their role over the last decade, ever since they were no longer solely employed in the Nursery. Supporting children across the 3–7 age range and beyond became the norm for many of them. Sometimes they were based in one class but often they spent time in a variety of classes each week. It was possible to visit several schools in the same district (as the author has) and see very different organizations and a variety of roles undertaken by nursery nurses. In some cases nursery nurses were almost like the teacher, involved in joint planning and teaching, undertaking many of the same tasks as teachers. In another school visited, the nursery nurses undertook mainly menial tasks such as laying out materials, cleaning up messy areas, mopping up after children, giving out milk and snacks, doing the photocopying and taking more of a care role with children. In many cases in the past, the wishes and capabilities of the post-holder would determine the role rather than any school management edict.

The name itself has connotations of days gone by when nurseries were perceived as 'safe' places with a cosy, soft and unchallenging atmosphere, somewhere to sleep and rest and listen to nursery rhymes. The development of practice and the advent of Sure Start early years provision, the integration of care and education for children up to 5 years old in centres such as Early Excellence Centres and now Children's Centres and, of course, the Foundation Stage developments have changed the nature and environment of early years settings to make them more vibrant and intellectually stimulating. This has meant a review and reconceptualization of roles, resulting in what Anning and Edwards (1999) termed 'the new professionals'. Further complications arise when we widen the lens to include the private and voluntary sector settings in the early years. There are few qualified teachers in the private and voluntary sector and many of the support workers have only the most basic qualifications, such as Level 1 National Vocational Qualifications in childcare. It will be interesting to monitor the effects that workforce reform and the regrading of posts in the state sector have on the private and voluntary sector. Will HLTAs appear in private nurseries?

●●● Working together and partnerships

To collaborate with some is often to shape up to confrontation with others. For collaboration is limited to those parts where good faith exists. (Fletcher and Adelman, 1981: 23).

Good faith is an essential component of collaborative working, and the openness and quality of relationships are of great importance to the success of any team. As identified in all the preceding chapters of this book, working together, collaboration, team working, partnerships and connecting with the other people in the classroom or school feature as key issues for successful support working in classrooms. Collaboration is not easy. It takes time, thoughtfulness and skill from all participants. Collaboration does not just 'happen'. As well as the tone of interpersonal relationships, the environment and 'hidden curriculum' send out messages. Bignold (in Chapter 2) stresses the importance of ethos and the physical layout of schools as having positive effects on both those who inhabit the space and those who visit. This may be a challenge for some people as this may mean a change in attitudes, beliefs and behaviour. She also highlights the need to value all those who contribute to children's learning and she identified the benefits of having support workers in school, whether voluntary or paid, who:

- foster children's self-esteem;
- acknowledge the cultural and linguistic backgrounds of all children;
- value what boys and girls can do equally (or men and women as in this example);
- foster an awareness of diversity in class, gender, ability and culture;
- promote respect for similarity and difference;
- challenge bias and prejudice;
- promote principles of inclusion and equity; and
- could provide a model for the community which supports the participation of the parents in children's learning (and other family members).

Benefits are also identified in Chapter 9 and it is strongly suggested that they need to be visible and celebrated in the school. Chapters 9 and 10 demonstrate how the voice of pupils or students about support for learning can be important in both understanding the roles and in supporting collaborative learning. Many support workers in schools have a 'history' with their school, as parent, relative or even as former pupil. Many educationalists extol this 'history' as a virtue. Hughes (in Chapter 4) illustrates how a learning mentor who is a member of the local community has 'street cred' with pupils and makes a valuable contribution to children's educational experience. Bignold (in Chapter 2) documents the value of a local community resident as a support worker in children's development in valuing diversity. There are, however, important ethical considerations in using local community, voluntary helpers or teachers and teaching assistants who are the parents of children at the school and who live in the local community. Having access to information about individual children's abilities, achievements, behaviour, special needs or other sensitive information through records and test results, classroom observation, staffroom or classroom discussion requires a professional code of behaviour. Where is this training for professional behaviour undertaken? This needs to be addressed in all forms of training for anyone who works with children in a voluntary or paid role. It also needs to be addressed in the settings themselves through clear policies and practices for all childcare workers, support workers and teachers. It is not difficult to imagine situations where the personal and professional interests collide to create ethical dilemmas for those who both work and live in the local community.

The DfEE guidance (2000: 24) regarding the effectiveness of the teamwork of teachers and teaching assistants emphazises the need for sharing plans and 'consultation over their execution'. Randall (2004) identified a general lack of quality time between teachers and teaching assistants in planning in her school. The problem that emerged was linked to the paid hours of employment of the teaching assistants and the workload of the teachers. Some teaching assistants may have timetabled preparation time when the teachers are not free. Releasing teachers to meet with their assistants during the day involves someone covering the class. Randall's further discussions with teachers involved in the action research project have indicated that they would rather plan with their assistants before or after school, but the assistants are not employed to work then. Relying on 'the goodwill of teachers and teaching assistants in meeting informally for planning and discussion' may not be good enough in the busy atmosphere of most schools.

In Chapter 7 the nursery nurse plays a significant role in the children's learning. The tensions inherent in a situation where an experienced and confident nursery nurse or support worker who has a high level of context-specific knowledge encounters a newly qualified teacher are illustrated, and these tensions demonstrate the complex issues about status, experience and collaborative work.

The importance of forming a good collaborative partnership between teacher and support worker is explicitly demonstrated in this tale. This scenario highlights the need for beginning teachers to work co-operatively with other adults and suggests teachers need to take the lead role in managing the involvement of other adults in the classroom. It also highlights the need for initial teacher education courses to accommodate training for this role even though the prescribed teacher education curriculum is arguably already over full.

●●● Role definition and description

The need to stress the importance of the clarification and development of the teaching assistants' role, [Moyles and Suschitzchy (1997)] is a finding corroborated by Randall's (2004) research. In her study, Randall asserted that there was total agreement about the need for clarification and development of the role of teaching assistants by the teacher and teaching assistant participants. The stages the teaching assistants went through in defining their role in terms of support for the pupil, teacher, curriculum and school revealed an overlap, confirming that the roles are 'not separate but interdependent' (DfEE, 2000). However, the guidelines, while adequate, fail to capture all the possible roles, concentrating on teaching rather than classroom support. This emphasizes the need to personalize job descriptions, allowing for the particular skills and abilities of the assistants. Randall's involvement with this process led her to concur with the DfEE that careful consideration needs to be given to the development of job descriptions with the associated implications of time and personnel.

Both headteachers interviewed in Chapter 10 emphasize the importance of clear, negotiated job descriptions for support staff. This, as they document, is not as easy as it may first seem. It is proving to be messy, inconsistent across the regions and difficult to understand and manage by unions who are centrally organized. The division of labour in educational contexts is arguably not as straightforward as it has been in the medical profession, although there are some who would argue differently. Issues of who does what are still being discussed, and the controversial area of whole-class 'teaching' by HLTAs still sits uneasily in most teachers' minds. They remember the 'Mums Army' debates of the past.

One of the thorny problems, which may cause more bureaucracy in schools, is having a teaching assistant with a variety of roles or job descriptions. For example, it would be possible to be a part-time support worker for children with special educational needs and a part-time HLTA, taking classes to release teachers for their PPA time. Or it could involve moving around the school in a support role for a particular subject such as ICT or sport. If a school had a number of these, the timetable arrangements would be complex indeed. Several flexible solutions to facilitate joint planning times are evident in Chapters 9 and 10: having a whole-school club afternoon run by teaching assistants or flexible starting times for teaching assistants so they can plan after-school hours with teachers. Creativity and flexibility are the order of the day for many schools as they strive to implement and develop collaborative support strategies. The current position with the various unions involved is also complex, with UNISON awaiting news of better pay and conditions for its members and headteachers' unions awaiting news of more money for schools. The position of the NUT has remained constant throughout: they have not signed up to the agreement. At some point this could potentially divide schools and destroy the collaboration needed to make remodelling of the workforce work. Good working relationships, as discussed above, are necessary to develop and implement policies and practices in schools. Bubb and Earley (2004) support good leadership and management strategies to facilitate a good work-life balance and workforce well being as essential to the success of schools in the future.

●●● Support for curriculum subjects

As stated in Chapter 6 and to a lesser extent in Chapter 8, confidence and competence in subject areas is an issue when teaching assistants are required to support children's learning. Subject knowledge has been for some time now a key issue for teachers themselves. The most common areas in primary schools are literacy, numeracy and ICT, although teaching assistants supporting children with special educational needs might find themselves supporting across the whole curriculum. Hall (in Chapter 3) lists the required abilities for teaching assistants, ranging from lateral thinking to patience and the ability to observe and evaluate progress. Although discussed in the context of special educational needs support, these seem suitable for all teaching assistants in schools.

Personal and pedagogical subject knowledge is key when working with individual or groups of children. What level of subject knowledge is required for teaching assistants? The answer is not clear. HLTAs must have English and maths GCSE-equivalent qualifications, but other teaching assistants need not. What kind of training in teaching numeracy and literacy will be the baseline for teaching assistants? Will there be curriculum specialist teaching assistants who only do ICT, for example? Clearly there is a huge training agenda.

●●● Professional development and training

In times of change and the development of new roles, it is important to consider support for professional development and training for those involved in the changes. Throughout the book this issue is addressed in different ways. Bignold (in Chapter 2) suggests that schools might like to organize whole-staff training to discuss and develop guidelines for welcoming 'special guests' from the community into school to support children. Certainly, the issue of Criminal Records Bureau clearance is one that she suggests has to be dealt with sensitively.

Hall (in Chapter 3) identifies greater reliance being placed on the use of teaching assistants and suggests that training and career development should be essential. However, Ofsted found that fewer than half of all LEAs provided relevant training for teaching assistants (www.inclusive.co.uk). Hall also suggests that all in-service workshops and sessions that seem relevant to the role of the teaching assistants should be available to them, or they should have regular in-school feedback from the teachers attending. She cautions that, if some teaching assistants attend courses and others do not, it is possible that a double layer of teaching assistants is created with a certain amount of prestige going to those who have attended.

In Chapter 4, Hughes refers to a National Training Programme for Learning Mentors, which was established in 2001. Materials for this programme have been updated and revised each year. Importantly, the programme provides learning mentors with a formal qualification.

In Chapters 5 and 6 (which focus on support for mathematics and ICT), knowledge of the subject matter is of great importance. Teachers and teaching assistants need regular subject updating and need to keep abreast of the pedagogical aspects specific to the subject in which they either teach or support children. Cronin and Bold in Chapter 5 do actually teach teaching assistants as part of their role and suggest a mind-mapping exercise to help understand the purposes of learning mathematics. They also suggest that teaching assistants need to explore and understand the frustration for some children in learning the subject and suggest shared planning as a good way to do this. Crowley and Richardson (in Chapter 6) think liaison with the ICT co-ordinator is essential to ensure continuity and to develop confidence. In their section on professional development they highlight the value of collaborative work and, in general, suggest many useful, practical activities.

Chapter 8 emphazises how teachers and student teachers need to learn together. Smith and Hewitt identify mentoring as a very worthwhile source of professional development for teachers and identify scenarios for student professional learning. There has been much research into mentoring (see Kerry and Shelton-Mayes, 1993; McIntyre *et al.*, 1993; Edwards and Collison,1996; Campbell and Kane, 1998), but still there is a need to explore the impact of mentoring on teachers' professional learning and development and the actual benefits for schools who are in partnership with teacher education institutions.

In Chapter 9 the voices of pupils and students provide a salutary reminder of the importance of consulting and listening to those who are supported and taught. They have a surprisingly clear view of what teachers and support workers do and should do. The headteacher in this chapter displays a good understanding and extensive experience of supporting and leading professional staff development. This serves to remind us of the importance of good leadership that is inclusive and that invites participation from all staff and from the pupils themselves.

The two headteachers interviewed in Chapter 10 have been involved in training as participants and as leaders of training for teachers and teaching assistants. They identify training as a key factor in the success of the workforce remodelling initiative and highlight the complexities of providing support and training for a diverse group of people. There are some difficult issues as the government's plans roll out. For example, what will the training for HLTAs finally look like and will it be sufficient for a role akin to a qualified teacher? What support and training will be required if a HLTA wants to take the Qualified Teacher route? Will there be training for student teachers to enable them to avoid the dilemmas that Jones describes in the Chapter 7 in her tale of the first encounters of an NQT and a nursery nurse?

There is currently a shift in government policy for continuing professional development towards school-based professional development for teachers. There is a recognition that teachers can learn from each other in inquiry-based learning, team teaching, focused discussion, joint planning and peer-coaching and mentoring situations (Campbell *et al.*, 2003). The opportunity to work and learn alongside each other is not just applicable to teachers. It can and should apply to a teaching assistant working with another teaching assistant and to teachers and teaching assistants working together. Good professional development should provide a balanced diet appropriate to the needs of the learners, and there are concerns that 'one size fits all' provision or lack of funding may result in poor-quality professional development (Campbell, 2003). Teachers and teaching assistants need to be vigilant and they need to articulate their needs. As Sachs (2003) advocated in her address to the British Educational Research Association in Edinburgh, educationalists need to become 'activists' in their profession, mobilizing for progress and development and asserting their rights.

There are many challenges and questions for the future, but there are also many opportunities. As this book goes to press the remodelling of the workforce is still a very contentious policy that is hotly debated. Let us hope that the challenges and opportunities can work collaboratively for a better future for children, teachers, support workers and schools.

●●● References

Anning, A. and Edwards, A. (1999) *Promoting Children's Learning from Birth to Five: Developing the New Early Years Professional.* Buckingham: Open University Press.

Bubb, S. and Earley, P. (2004) *Managing Teacher Workload: Work-Life Balance and Wellbeing,* London: Paul Chapman.

Campbell, A. (2003) 'Teachers' research and professional development in England: some questions, issues and concerns', *Journal of In-service Education.* 29 (3): 375–88.

Campbell, A., Hustler, D. and McNamara, O. (2003) 'Researching continuing professional development: the use of fictional pen portraits to illustrate and analyse teachers' perceptions and experiences'. *Professional Development Today.* 7, (2) Spring 2004, 13–19.

Campbell, A. and Kane, I. (1998) *School-based Teacher Education: Telling Tales from a Fictional Primary School.* London: David Fulton.

DfEE (2000) *Working with Teaching Assistants: A Good Practice Guide.* London: DfEE Publications.

Edwards, A. and Collison, J. (1996) *Mentoring and Developing Practice in Primary Schools: Supporting Student Learning in Schools.* Milton Keynes: Open University Press.

Fletcher, C. and Adelman, C. (1981) 'Collaboration as a research process', *Journal of Community Education,* 1 (1), 23–33.

Kerry, T. and Shelton-Mayes, A. (eds) (1993) *Issues in Mentoring.* London: Routledge.

McIntyre, D., Hagger, H. and Wilkin, M. (1993) *Mentoring: Perspectives on School-based Teacher Education.* London: Kogan Page.

Moyles, J. and Suschitzky, W. (1997) 'Jills of all trades?… Classroom assistants in KS1 classes', London: Association of Teachers and Lecturers Publications.

Randall, H. (2004) 'An investigation into some strategies for enhancing the role of teaching assistants in a Liverpool primary school.' Unpublished MEd dissertation, Liverpool Hope University.

Sachs, J. (2003) 'Teacher activism: mobilising the profession.' Plenary address, BERA conference, Edinburgh.

●●● Index